FILET CROCHET
Projects and Charted Designs

Edited by
Mrs. F. W. Kettelle

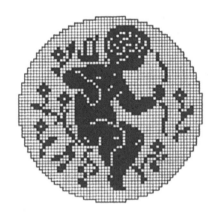

Dover Publications, Inc.
New York

FIG. 1. TEA CLOTH IN FANCY FILET CROCHET. (See pages 44 and 45)

PUBLISHER'S NOTE

Filet crochet patterns are meant to be worked from a photograph or a chart; detailed instructions are normally not required. This book was reprinted directly from a Priscilla needlework booklet, first published in 1915, and is complete in its present form. Dover does not have any additional material in the form of charts or written instructions. If you encounter trouble following one of the photographs, try enlarging it on a xerox machine or charting it yourself on graph paper.

This Dover edition, first published in 1979, is an unabridged republication of the work first published by the Priscilla Publishing Company in 1915 under the title *The Priscilla Filet Crochet Book No. 2. A Collection of Beautiful Designs in Filet Crochet Introducing Filet Crochet Brodé, Embroidery on Crochet and Cameo Crochet.*

International Standard Book Number

ISBN-13: 978-0-486-23745-9
ISBN-10: 0-486-23745-1

Manufactured in the United States by Courier Corporation
23745116   2014
www.doverpublications.com

FILET CROCHET

Filet Crochet takes its name from Filet Brodé which it resembles. It is at its very best when done with fine thread and the finest needle, yet it is handsome in coarse thread. For the best effect, the crochet must be firmly and evenly done.

MATERIALS.—Any good thread is suitable. In the list below the size of Cordonnet crochet cotton is given with the size of hook and the number of meshes in an inch of the work. As the size of crochet varies with the worker, the number of spaces given is only approximate.

No. of Cotton	No. of Hook	Meshes to Inch	No. of Cotton	No. of Hook	Meshes to Inch
1	4	3	40	11	7
2	9	4	50	12	7½
3	9	4	60	12	8
5	9	4½	70	14	8½
10	9	5	80	14	8½
20	11	6	100	14	9
30	11	6½	150	14	10

EXPLANATION OF TERMS.—Chain (ch). With a slip knot on the needle, pull a loop through, then a loop through that, etc.

Slip stitch (sl). A loop on the hook, hook through work, pull loop through both.

Single crochet (s c). A loop on the hook, pull loop through work, pull loop through the two loops.

Double crochet (d). A loop on the hook, thread over hook once, pull a loop through work, loop through two loops, loop through remaining two.

Treble crochet (t). A loop on the hook, thread over hook twice, pull a loop through work, crochet off in twos.

Double treble (d t). A loop on the hook, thread over hook three times, pull a loop through work, crochet off in twos.

Space or mesh (s or sp). Chain 2, miss 2 sts of foundation, 1 d in next.

To add meshes at the beginning of a row work the required number of ch, plus 5 for turning, and proceed as usual.

The method of adding open meshes at the end of a row is as follows: Chain 2, a d t, joining where the last d was joined. Each succeeding d t is fastened under 2 threads in the middle of the preceding d t.

Puff stitch (see Figs. 31 and 32). A d in top of d below, 6 d in space below, join top of seventh d to top of second d with a sl st on wrong side of work, a d in top of next d below. Care must be taken to have all puffs on same side of work.

Picot (p). Chain 6, sl in first of chain.

EXPLANATION OF TABLES.—Tabulated directions are used for some of the designs, as they save space, and many workers find them easier to follow than the usual directions. Each horizontal row of figures stands for one entire row of crochet. Every row is to be read from left to right. When you come to the end of a row of figures, turn your crochet. The letters at the top of each column tell what the numbers in that column represent. "S" means "spaces." "D" means "double crochet." The foundation chain is always three times the number of spaces in the first row, plus six. For example, in the pattern, Fig. 4, the first row has 35 spaces or meshes; therefore, chain 111, turn. The first four rows read as follows:

1st row—Make 1 d in the ninth chain from hook, * ch 2, miss 2 stitches of foundation, 1 d in next. Repeat from * until 35 spaces are made. Chain 5, turn.

2d row—Same as 1st row.

3d row—Two sp, 4 d, 7 sp, 19 d, 10 sp, 4 d, 8 sp, turn.

4th row—Five sp, 4 d, 1 sp, 4 d, 1 sp, 4 d, 1 sp, 4 d, 6 sp, 7 d, 4 sp, 10 d, 2 sp, 13 d, 2 sp.

From this, it will be seen that no attention is paid to blocks (solid mesh), although you can prove up your work in this way. Each single block consists of 4 d. Two or more blocks consist of three times the number of blocks plus 1. Always make 5 chain in turning. This makes the first space. When the row begins with d, use three chain for turning.

REFERENCE LETTERS USED IN TABLES. — Special reference letters are sometimes used in tabulated directions, and their meanings are as follows:

E.—Slip stitch over one space or four d.

W.—Chain 8, turn, 1 d in fourth ch from hook.

X.—Used to fill squares that would otherwise be left blank; the use of the letter prevents confusion.

F.—This means a "festoon" which is made as follows: Chain 3, miss 2 stitches of foundation, s c in next stitch, ch 3, miss 2 stitches of foundation, d in next stitch.

B.—Block. Chain 5, miss 5 stitches of foundation, d in next stitch; blocks are usually combined with festoons.

A neat way of finishing a triangular piece of Filet Crochet is with triangular meshes on the oblique edge. On the end of a row this may be done by joining with a t instead of 2 ch and d. For the beginning of a row, 3 chain are made for turning instead of the ordinary 5 chain. See also the directions for Fig. 55, page 20.

We are aware that some workers in Filet Crochet do not depend on directions, but prefer to follow an illustration of the finished work. It will be found that a number of the designs in this book have been arranged to meet the preference of such workers.

Unless the edge is of d, it is a good plan to reinforce the edge with a row of s c, put [CONCLUDED ON PAGE 40]

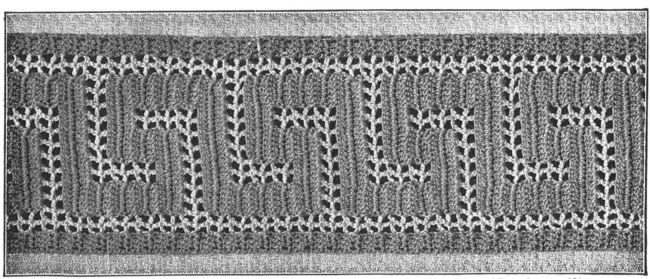

FIG. 2. CAMEO CROCHET INSERTION FOR TOWEL. FULL SIZE. (See Figs. 106, 107, and page 40)

FIG. 3. CENTREPIECE. (See Table, Fig. 4.) 35 meshes

Figure 3. CENTREPIECE. — Use No. 40 linen thread and No. 11 hook. Take a piece of linen 18 inches square and pin on the completed corners. Mark the outline of the crochet with a basting thread, and cut out the corners, allowing ¼ inch for a hem. After the corners are sewn in, work a row of spaces around the piece; finish the edge with a row of single crochet, a picot at every fifth space. These corners may be used for a table-runner or bureau-scarf, by using a strip of linen of the desired length. In a runner, the crochet should be inserted so that the rows of work are parallel to the ends of the piece. Four tassels at each end make a pretty finish for a piece of this description.

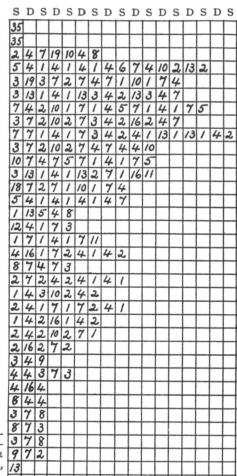

FIG. 4. TABULATED DIRECTIONS FOR CENTREPIECE, FIG. 3

S	D	S	D	S	D	S	D	S	D	S	D	S	D	S	D	S
35																
35																
2	4	7	19	10	4	8										
5	4	1	4	1	4	1	4	6	7	4	10	2	13	2		
3	19	3	7	2	7	4	7	1	10	1	7	4				
3	13	1	4	1	13	3	4	2	13	3	4	7				
7	4	2	10	1	7	1	4	5	7	1	4	1	7	5		
3	7	2	10	2	7	3	4	2	16	2	4	7				
7	7	1	4	1	7	3	4	2	4	1	13	1	13	1	4	2
3	7	2	10	2	7	4	7	4	4	10						
10	7	4	7	5	7	1	4	1	7	5						
3	13	1	4	1	13	2	7	1	16	11						
18	7	2	7	1	10	1	7	4								
5	4	1	4	1	4	1	4	7								
1	13	5	4	8												
12	4	1	7	3												
1	7	1	4	1	7	11										
4	16	1	7	2	4	1	4	2								
8	7	4	7	3												
2	7	2	4	2	4	1	4	1								
1	4	3	10	2	4	2										
2	4	1	7	1	7	2	4	1								
1	4	2	16	1	4	2										
2	4	2	10	2	7	1										
2	16	2	7	2												
3	4	9														
4	4	3	7	3												
4	16	4														
8	4	4														
3	7	8														
8	7	3														
3	7	8														
9	7	2														
13																
13																

FIG. 5. (No. 30 linen thread and No. 11 hook) 157 x 113 meshes

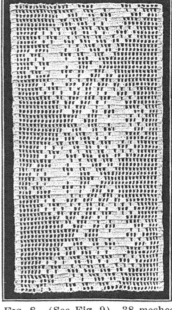

FIG. 8. (See Fig. 9) 38 meshes

FIG. 6. PILLOW. (See block pattern, pages 6 and 7, Fig. 11)

In this pillow the crochet is done with No. 30 Cordonnet crochet cotton and No. 11 hook, and is inserted in a narrow frame of linen. The edge may be finished with bobbin lace or an edging of filet crochet. Attention is called to the two beautiful panels, Fig. 63, "Spring," page 24, and Fig. 69, "Autumn," page 26. These designs would make attractive pillows, and could be made up in the same way as the Peacock design.

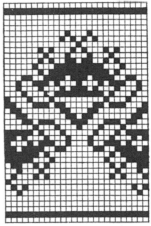

Fig. 9   (See Fig. 8)

FIG. 7. CHURCH LACE   64 meshes

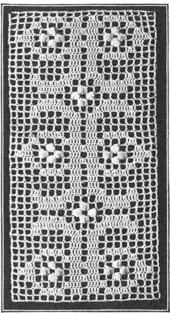

FIG. 10.   19 meshes

Fig. 11. (See Fig. 6)

127 x 178 meshes

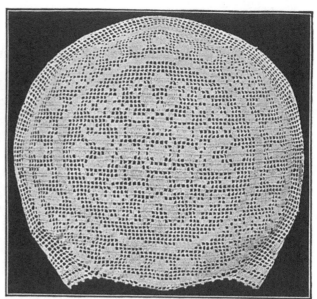

FIG. 13.   BABY'S CAP, BACK VIEW.   (See Fig. 14)

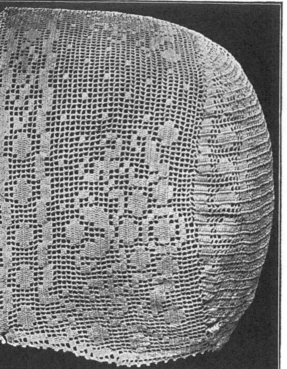

FIG. 12.   BABY'S CAP, SIDE VIEW.   (See Fig. 15)

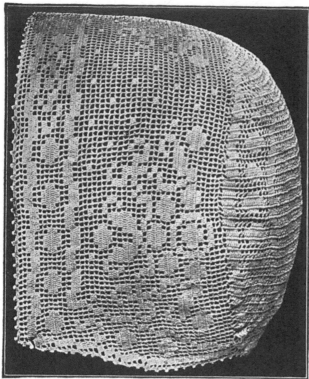

FIG. 14.   HALF OF CROWN OF BABY'S CAP.   (See Fig. 13.)   Commence crown at X; chain 36, double in ninth chain, etc. When B is reached, make the last half like the first half. Materials.—One ball Cordonnet crochet cotton No. 150, hook No. 14.

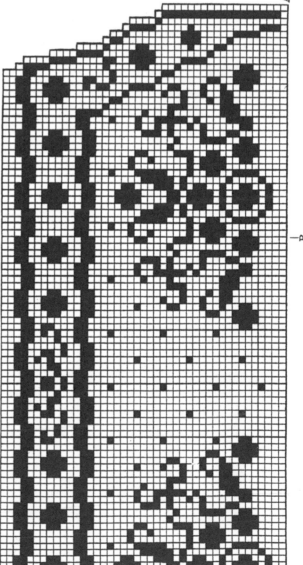

FIG. 15.   HALF OF FRONT OF BABY'S CAP.   (See Fig. 12.)   Start the front at A on the crown.

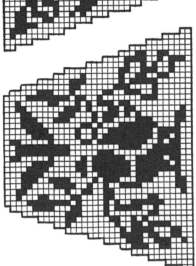

Figure 16. **CANDLE-SHADE.** — The four block patterns for this shade are given on this page (see Fig. 17). Use No. 60 Cordonnet crochet cotton and No. 12 hook. The four sides are sewed together by the slanting edges, leaving all the short sides together at the top, the upper and lower edges are finished with single crochet, having a group of five picots in place of every tenth stitch.

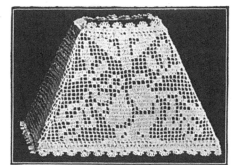

FIG. 16. CANDLE-SHADE (See Fig. 17)

FIG. 18. Centrepiece, 28 Inches Square. (See Figs. 19, 20)
Use No. 70 cotton and No. 14 hook

FIG. 17. PATTERNS OF FOUR SIDES OF CANDLE-SHADE. (See Fig. 16)

FIG. 19. (See Fig. 18.) 26 meshes. Work 2¾ x 11 inches

FIG. 20. (See Fig. 18.) 43 meshes Work, 4½ inches Square

FIG. 21

34 meshes

Figure 21. CENTREPIECE. NEZ PERCE DESIGN. *Materials.*—Two balls Cordonnet crochet cotton No. 30; hook No. 11.

For the linen centre, trace a circle on a firm piece of linen, using a ten-inch plate, stitch along the line thus traced with the machine three times, then cut the linen close to the stitching and cover with very close single crochet (s c). Upon this work the pattern.

1st row—Double (d), with 1 chain (ch) between in every stitch (st) around. The model has 277 spaces (sp).

2d row—Double in each d and d in each ch of previous row. *3d row*—Double in every other d of 2d row with 2 ch between d. (These ch must be worked tightly.)

4th to 10th rows—Same as 3d row.

11th row—Widen circle by making 4 sp over the first 3 sp of previous row, then 6 sp over 6 sp; repeat all around.

12th row—Count number of sp in 11th row and divide by 8, to begin design. The number will depend upon the number of s c it took for foundation around edge of linen. The model has 300 sp, divided by 8 equals 37 and 38 sp for each motif, or 2 sp for top of design and 36 and 35 sp, respectively, between motifs. This row reads: 19 sp, 7 d, 36 sp, 7 d, 35 sp, 7 d, 36 sp, 7 d, 35 sp, 7 d, 36 sp, 7 d, 35 sp, 7 d, 36 sp, 7 d, 16 sp.

13th row—Work sp to within 1 sp of motif, then make 13 d (7 d over 7 d and 3 d to right and left of 7 d); repeat around. *14th row*—Work to within 2 sp of motif, then make 25 d; repeat around.

15th row—Work to within 2 sp of motif and make 13 d, 5 sp (d in every other d with 2 ch between, increasing the circle), 13 d, finishing 2 sp to left of motif. Between each motif widen 3 times by placing 3 sp over 2 at beginning and end of motif and midway between.

16th row—Work to within 2 sp of motif and make 16 d, 7 sp, 16 d; repeat around.

17th row—Work to within 2 sp of motif and make 19 d, 9 sp, 19 d; repeat around.

18th row—Work to motif and make 5 sp over 15 d, 4 d, 9 sp, 4 d; repeat around.

19th row—Work to within 1 sp of d of last row and make 10 d, 7 sp, 10 d; repeat around.

20th row—Work to within 2 sp of motif and make 19 d, 5 sp, 19 d; repeat around.

21st row—Work to within 2 sp of motif and make 28 d, 3 sp, 28 d; repeat around.

22d row—Work to motif and 9 sp over 28 d, then 10 d over 3 sp, and 9 sp more over 28 d of last row; repeat around.

23d row—Work to within 1 sp of motif and make 16 d (covering 10 d of 22d row and 1 sp to right and left). Between each motif in this row widen 3 times by placing 4 sp over 3; repeat around.

24th row—Work to within 1 sp of motif and make 22 d; repeat around.

25th row—Work to within 1 sp of motif and make 28 d; repeat around.

26th row—Work sp all around, widen once over each motif and once between.

27th row—Space all around. *28th row*—Space all around.

29th row—Five sp over 5 sp, then 5 d over next sp; repeat around. *30th row*—Same as 29th row.

31st row—Three sp over 3 sp and 11 d over next 2 sp and 5 d of 30th row; repeat around.

32d row—One sp, 18 d (7 over 2 sp and 11 more d, adding 1 d and widening for last time); repeat around.

33d row—Double all around.

34th row—Spaces all around.

SHELL FOR EDGE.—Chain 3, 3 d in same place, fasten with slip stitch to top of next d of last row, ch 3; repeat around.

Figure 22. PILLOW. — Use No. 20 Cordonnet crochet cotton and No. 11 hook. Chain (ch) 270, turn.

1st row—Double crochet (d) in 10th from hook, 1 space (sp), (ch 2, miss 2, d in next), 7 d (including d after sp), * 2 sp, 7 d; repeat from * 20 times more (22 blocks of 7 d). Chain 3, turn.

2d row—Miss 1 d, 6 d in next 6, * 2 sp, 7 d; repeat from *, ending row with 2 sp, ch 3, turn.

3d row—Six d, 2 sp, * ch 10, miss 2 sp, 2 sp over next 7 d; repeat from *, having 20 chs of 10, after last 2 sp, make 6 d over 2 sp at end row, ch 3, turn.

4th row—Six d, 1 sp, * ch 2, miss 1 of 10 ch, 7 single crochet (s c) in next 7 of ch, ch 2, d in d between next 2 sp; repeat from *, making 7 d at end, ch 5, turn.

5th row—Miss 3 d, d in next, 1 sp, * ch 10, d in next s c, 2 sp over 7 s c; repeat from * with 7 d at end, ch 3, turn. *6th row*—Like 4th row, ending with 2 sp.

Work 2 more rows with clusters of 4 sp, and 1 large sp, alternating. End each row with 7 d.

In *9th row*—After 2d ch of 10 make * 2 sp, 7 d; repeat 14 times, 2 sp, end row as before.

In *10th row*—Work large sp as shown, then 7 d and 2 sp over those of last row, finish with large sp as before.

From this point directions for the border will be omitted and only the design of spaces and double crochet inside of the blocks of border will be given. These will not include any spaces between the blocks of straight edge.

11th row—Fifty-four sp. *12th row*—Fifty-four sp. *13th row*—Twenty-three sp, 10 d, 7 sp, 7 d, 5 sp, 16 d, 7 sp.

14th row—Six sp, 4 d, 5 sp, 4 d, 3 sp, 4 d, 2 sp, 4 d, 6 sp, 10 d, 14 sp, 4 d, 3 sp, 4 d, 4 sp.

15th row—Three sp, 10 d, 1 sp, 4 d, 13 sp, 4 d, 2 sp, 4 d, 2 sp, 4 d, 4 sp, 4 d, 3 sp, 4 d, 1 sp, 4 d, 4 sp, 4 d, 2 sp, 4 d, 3 sp.

16th row—Three sp, 4 d, 1 sp, 4 d, 1 sp, 4 d, 4 sp, 7 d, 9 sp, 4 d, 1 sp, 4 d, 1 sp, 4 d, 13 sp, 4 d, 2 sp, 7 d, 4 sp.

17th row—Six sp, 4 d, 2 sp, 4 d, 4 sp, 7 d, 2 sp, 7 d, 2 sp, 4 d, 3 sp, 4 d, 2 sp, 7 d, 5 sp, 4 d, 5 sp, 4 d, 3 sp, 4 d, 1 sp.

18th row—Two sp, 10 d, 3 sp, 13 d, 1 sp, 7 d, 4 sp, 4 d, 1 sp, 4 d, 1 sp, 4 d, 1 sp, 4 d, 1 sp, 4 d, 6 sp, 4 d, 1 sp, 4 d, 1 sp, 4 d, 1 sp, 4 d, 2 sp, 4 d, 4 sp.

19th row—Three sp, 4 d, 1 sp, 4 d, 2 sp, 13 d, 1 sp, 7 d, 8 sp, 10 d, 8 sp, 10 d, 3 sp, 4 d, 5 sp.

20th row—Five sp, 4 d, 4 sp, 10 d, 5 sp, 22 d, 6 sp, 7 d, 1 sp, 19 d, 6 sp.

21st row—Eight sp, 16 d, 2 sp, 4 d, 2 sp, 10 d, 1 sp, 16 d, 1 sp, 10 d, 2 sp, 7 d, 3 sp, 7 d, 4 sp.

22d row—Ten sp, 7 d, 2 sp, 10 d, 1 sp, 10 d, 1 sp, 10 d, 2 sp, 7 d, 1 sp, 22 d, 7 sp.

23d row—Ten sp, 13 d, 1 sp, 7 d, 3 sp, 7 d, 1 sp, 10 d, 1 sp, 7 d, 3 sp, 4 d, 9 sp.

24th row—Ten sp, 4 d, 2 sp, 7 d, 1 sp, 10 d, 1 sp, 7 d, 3 sp, 19 d, 1 sp, 10 d, 7 sp.

25th row—Six sp, 4 d, 1 sp, 10 d, 2 sp, 4 d, 1 sp, 7 d, 3 sp, 7 d, 1 sp, 10 d, 1 sp, 7 d, 2 sp, 4 d, 8 sp.

26th row—Nine sp, 4 d, 1 sp, 7 d, 1 sp, 10 d, 1 sp, 7 d, 1 sp, 7 d, 1 sp, 19 d, 3 sp, 4 d, 6 sp.

27th row—Eleven sp, 13 d, 3 sp, 4 d, 2 sp, 7 d, 1 sp, 4 d, 1 sp, 7 d, 2 sp, 4 d, 7 sp.

28th row—Seven sp, 4 d, 4 sp, 4 d, 1 sp, 4 d, 3 sp, 4 d, 1 sp, 4 d, 1 sp, 4 d, 15 sp.

29th row—Six sp, 4 d, 3 sp, 4 d, 4 sp, 7 d, 1 sp, 4 d, 1 sp, 7 d, 2 sp, 4 d, 4 sp, 4 d, 6 sp.

30th row—Seven sp, 13 d, 1 sp, 7 d, 2 sp, 4 d, 1 sp, 4 d, 5 sp, 7 d, 3 sp, 4 d, 6 sp.

31st row—Seven sp, 4 d, 2 sp, 19 d, 2 sp, 4 d, 1 sp, 4 d, 13 sp.

32d row—Nine sp, 13 d, 2 sp, 4 d, 1 sp, 19 d, 1 sp, 4 d, 4 sp, 4 d, 4 sp. *33d row*—Five sp, 10 d, 1 sp, 7 d, 5 sp, 4 d, 2 sp, 4 d, 1 sp, 4 d, 2 sp, 4 d, 7 sp.

34th row—Seven sp, 4 d, 2 sp, 4 d, 1 sp, 4 d, 1 sp, 4 d, 1 sp, 25 d, 4 sp, 7 d, 2 sp. *35th row*—One sp, 16 d, 1 sp, 31 d, 1 sp, 4 d, 2 sp, 13 d, 5 sp.

36th row—Four sp, 4 d, 5 sp, 4 d, 1 sp, 4 d, 1 sp, 25 d, 4 sp, 7 d, 2 sp. *37th row*—Five sp, 10 d, 1 sp, 7 d, 5 sp, 4 d, 2 sp, 4 d, 8 sp.

38th row—Eight sp, 4 d, 2 sp, 19 d, 1 sp, 4 d, 4 sp, 4 d, 4 sp. *39th row*—Seven sp, 4 d, 2 sp, 19 d, 3 sp, 4 d, 6 sp. *40th row*—Seven sp, 4 d, 6 sp, 7 d, 3 sp, 4 d, 6 sp.

41st row—Six sp, 4 d, 3 sp, 4 d, 4 sp, 10 d, 6 sp.

42d row—Nine sp, 7 d, 13 sp. *43d row*—Three sp, 4 d, 7 sp, 7 d, 9 sp. *44th row*—Ten sp, 10 d, 1 sp, 4 d, 4 sp, 4 d, 2 sp, 4 d. *45th row*—Two sp, 4 d, 4 sp, 16 d, 8 sp.

46th row—Ten sp, 7 d, 4 sp, 4 d, 3 sp. *47th row*—Four sp, 16 d, 9 sp. *48th row*—Ten sp, 4 d, 1 sp, 4 d, 5 sp.

49th row—Four sp, 4 d, 2 sp, 4 d, 2 sp, 4 d, 5 sp.

50th row—Five sp, 4 d, 2 sp, 4 d, 3 sp, 4 d, 3 sp.

51st row—Two sp, 4 d, 5 sp, 7 d, 4 sp. *52d row*—Eleven sp, 4 d, 2 sp. *53d row*—Two sp, 4 d, 2 sp, 7 d, 5 sp.

54th row—Four sp, 4 d, 2 sp, 4 d, 1 sp, 4 d, 2 sp.

55th row—Two sp, 4 d, 2 sp, 4 d, 1 sp, 4 d, 2 sp.

56th row—Two sp, 4 d, 3 sp, 4 d, 3 sp. *57th row*—Four sp, 10 d, 1 sp. *58th row*—Eight sp. *59th row*—Six sp.

60th row—Six sp. *61st row*—Four sp. *62d row*—Four sp.

Continue the border as shown until it reaches a point, making 7 d in last 2 rows.

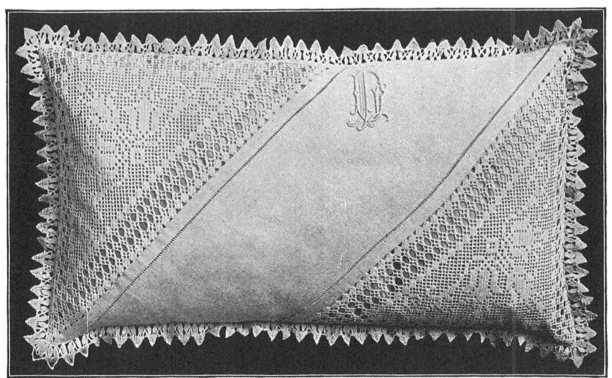

FIG. 22. SOFA PILLOW. (See directions for working on this page)

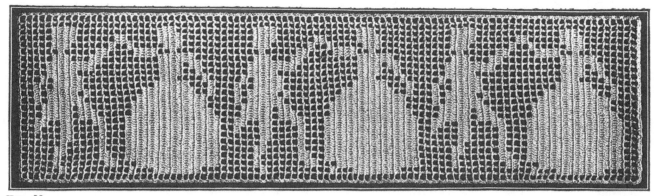

FIG. 23

24 meshes

FIG. 24. TEA CLOTH. (See Directions and Details on page 13)

Figure 24. TEA CLOTH. — Embroidery and crochet are very attractively combined in this handsome cloth. The diagram (Fig. 25) gives the measurements of the cloth, and the crochet can be easily carried out by the aid of the details. The embroidery is worked with cotton in satin-stitch. For the crochet use No. 30 Cordonnet crochet cotton and a No. 11 hook.

To crochet the insertion, chain 11. The first row consists of 7 d (see Fig. 26), every other row being widened two meshes at each end. For widening at the beginning of a row, ch 8, turn, allowing 3 ch for 1 d, work 1 d into each of the next 5 ch and the last of the preceding row, 7 d in all. To add solid meshes at the end of a row, when there is no foundation on which to work, treble are used, the first t being fastened into the same place as the last d in the row, and each succeeding t fastened through two loops at the bottom of the preceding t, 6 t being made in all. The 25th row begins at C (see diagram, Fig. 25) and ends at D. At this point it would be well to compare the crochet with working model (Fig. 26). Complete two sides of the diamond, ending at E. Figure 27 shows the corner. Cut thread, join at F and work the other two sides of the diamond like the first two, ending at G. Join G and E with 11 ch. Cut thread and join two spaces from the end of the line at H. Work the final triangular piece like the first, completing the insertion.

The illustration is a sufficient guide for working the edging, but the beginner will need directions for the corner. It will prevent confusion if the crochet is begun with the first row of this detail (Fig. 29) and the corner made first.

The pattern begins with the row marked A in Fig. 28, and it will help to compare the crochet with working model, Fig. 29, as the work proceeds.

1st row—Chain 60, turn, 2 spaces (sp), 16 d, 4 sp, 10 d, 2 sp, 7 d.

2d row—Slip stitch back over 4 d of the seven in last row, 7 d, 7 sp, 4 d, 7 sp.

3d row—Six sp, 4 d, 1 sp, 16 d, 2 sp, 7 d.

4th row—Slip stitch back over 4 d, 7 d, 2 sp, 10 d, 2 sp, 4 d, 5 sp.

5th row—Five sp, 4 d, 4 sp, 7 d, 2 sp, 7 d, ch 5.

6th row—Seven d, 2 sp, 4 d, 4 sp, 4 d, 4 sp.

7th row—Three sp, 4 d, 1 sp, 4 d. 6 sp, 7 d, ch 5.

8th row—Seven d, 4 sp, 7 d, 1 sp, 4 d, 1 sp, 4 d, 1 sp.

9th row—Four d, 3 sp, 13 d, 3 sp, 7 d.

10th row—Seven d, 2 sp, 4 d, 1 sp, 10 d, 2 sp.

11th row—Three sp, 4 d, 2 sp, 4 d, 2 sp, 7 d.

12th row—Slip stitch back over 4 d, 7 d, 1 sp, 10 d, 2 sp.

13th row—Six sp, 7 d. *14th row*—Seven d, 3 sp.

15th row—Three sp, 7 d. *16th row*—Slip stitch back over 4 d, 4 d, 1 sp.

17th row—Seven d. *18th row*—Slip stitch back over the 7 d just made, ch 5, 7 d (these are made at right angles to those made so far, the last three are fastened in the side of the row of 7 d instead of along the top). Fasten a

d in the side of the step forming a space, ch 2, fasten a d in the corner of the step. This forms the first space on the next row.

19th row—Seven d, ch 5. *20th row*—Seven d, 3 sp, ch 2, fasten to middle of step, slip stitch up to corner.

21st row—Nine d, 1 sp, 7 d, ch 5.

22d row—Seven d, 2 sp, 4 d, 2 sp, 4 d, ch 2, fasten to middle of step, slip stitch up to corner.

23d row—Nine d, 1 sp, 4 d, 2 sp, 7 d.

24th row—Seven d, 3 sp, 13 d, 1 sp, a d in middle of next step, ch 2, a d in corner.

25th row—Four d, 1 sp, 7 d, 4 sp, 7 d.

26th row—Slip stitch back over 4 d, 7 d, 7 sp, 4 d, 1 sp, a d in middle of next step, ch 2, a d in corner.

27th row—Four d, 1 sp, 16 d, 2 sp, 7 d.

28th row—Slip stitch back over 4 d, 7 d, 2 sp, 10 d, 2 sp, 4 d, 2 sp, a d in middle of next step, ch 2, a d in corner.

29th row—Two sp, 4 d, 4 sp, 7 d, 1 sp, 7 d, ch 5.

30th row—Seven d, 2 sp, 4 d, 5 sp, 4 d, 4 sp, ch 2, fasten to corner, sl forward one space. *31st row*—Seven sp, 4 d, 7 sp, 7 d, ch 5. *32d row*—Seven d, 6 sp, 7 d, 8 sp. From here work by the illustration, Fig. 24.

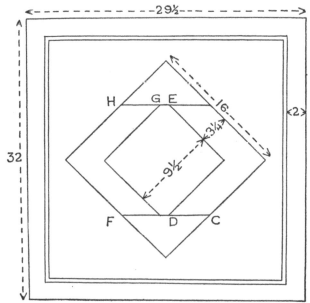

FIG. 25. DIAGRAM OF TEA CLOTH ON PAGE 12

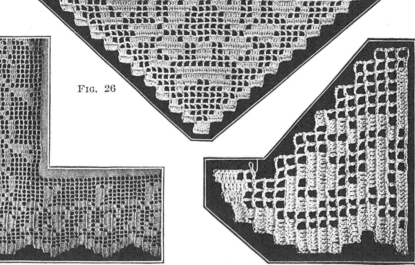

FIG. 26

FIG. 27

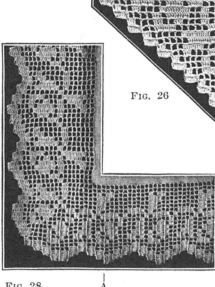

FIG. 28

A

FIG. 29

13

FIG. 30   33 meshes   FIG. 31. (See Puff Stitch, page 3)   15 meshes

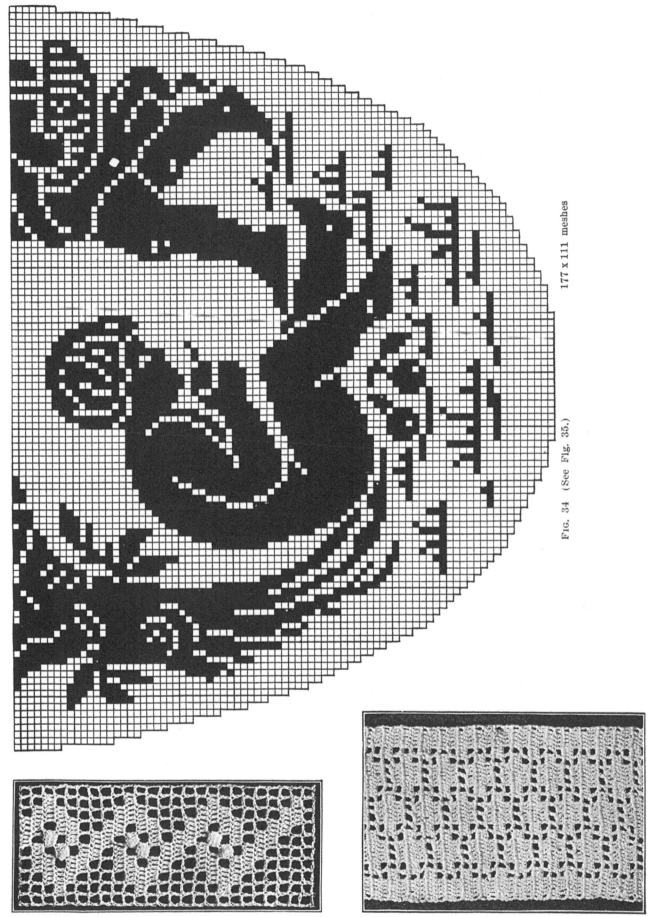

177 x 111 meshes

FIG. 34 (See Fig. 35.)

FIG. 32. (See directions for Puff Stitch on page 3.) 10 meshes

FIG. 33   18 meshes

15

FIG. 35. (See Fig. 34)

TRAY. — The crochet model was done with No. 100 crochet cotton and No. 14 hook. The work measures 10 x 15 inches.

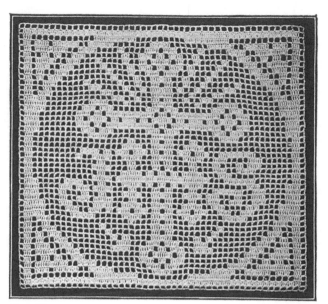

FIG. 36   49 meshes

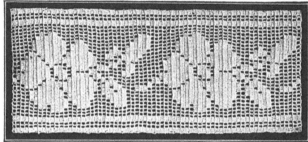

FIG. 37. (See Fig. 40)

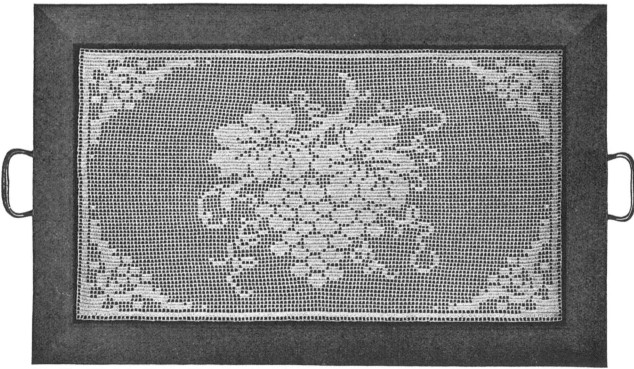

FIG. 38. (Worked with No. 70 Cordonnet crochet cotton and No. 14 hook)   129 x 77 meshes

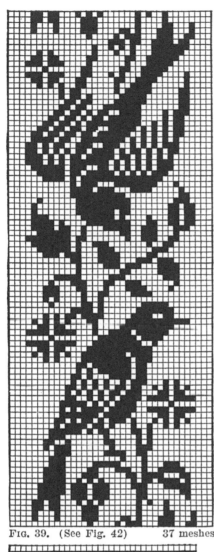

FIG. 39. (See Fig. 42)   37 meshes

FIG. 42. (See Fig. 39)

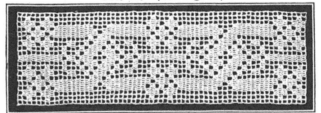

FIG. 43.   19 meshes

FIG. 40. (See Fig. 37)   32 meshes

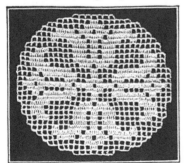

FIG. 41.   29 meshes

FIG. 44. (Model worked with No. 50 Cordonnet crochet cotton and No. 12 hook)   85 meshes

17

Figure 48. LAMP-SHADE.—This shade is made of linen, with eyelet embroidery and inserts of filet crochet. The patterns of the three medallions and six triangles are given (see Figs. 49 and 51), and the crochet was done with No. 60 Cordonnet crochet cotton and No. 12 hook.

The shade is 39 inches around and 7¾ inches high, and is trimmed with bobbin lace, tassels, and crochet pendants. The lining is of colored silk.

FIG. 48.   LAMP-SHADE.   (See Figs. 49, 51)

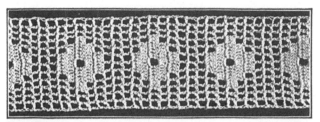

FIG. 45   12 meshes

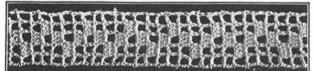

FIG. 46   5 meshes

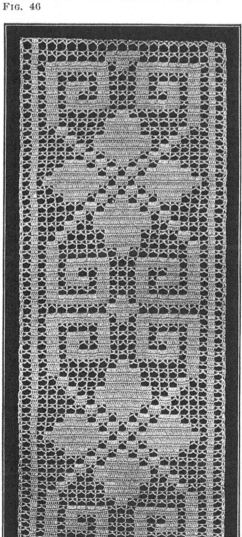

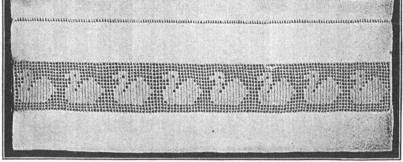

FIG. 49.   (See Fig. 48)   62 meshes

FIG. 47   40 meshes FIG. 50. (No. 60 cotton, No. 12 hook)   15 meshes

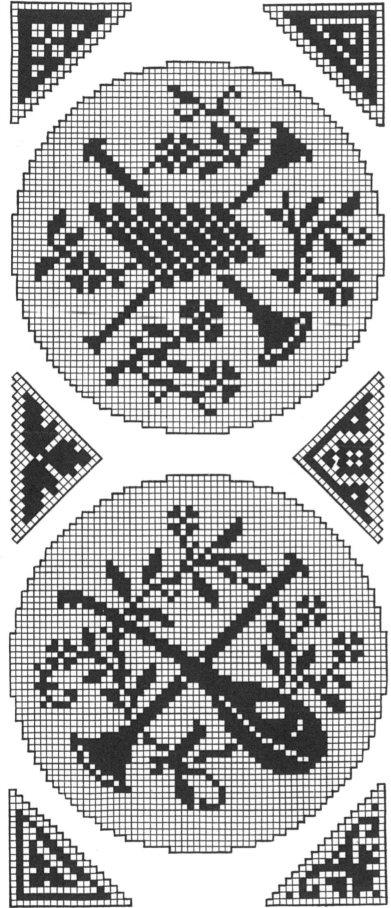

FIG. 52. (See Fig. 53) 20 meshes

S	D	S	D	S	D	S	D	S	D	S	D
X	4	F	4	12	4	F	4				
X	4	B	4	5	7	5	4	B	4		
1	10	5	4	2	4	5	10	1			
X	4	F	4	3	4	2	4	5	4	F	4
X	4	B	4	8	4	3	4	B	4		
1	10	4	4	4	7	3	10	1			
X	4	F	4	1	13	3	4	3	4	F	4
X	4	B	4	4	4	2	13	1	4	B	4
1	10	3	7	2	4	6	10	1			
X	4	F	4	6	4	6	4	5	4	F	4
X	4	B	4	2	10	1	10	3	4	B	4
1	10	3	13	1	13	2	10	1			
X	4	F	4	2	7	8	7	3	4	F	4

FIG. 53. (See Fig. 52)

The groups of 10 d at the edges of this strip are all fastened into the block, where it is usual to fasten only seven.

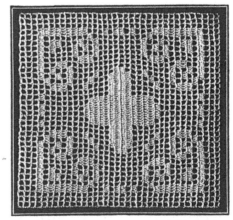

FIG. 51. EIGHT BLOCK PATTERNS FOR LAMP-SHADE. (See Fig. 48)

FIG. 54   36 meshes

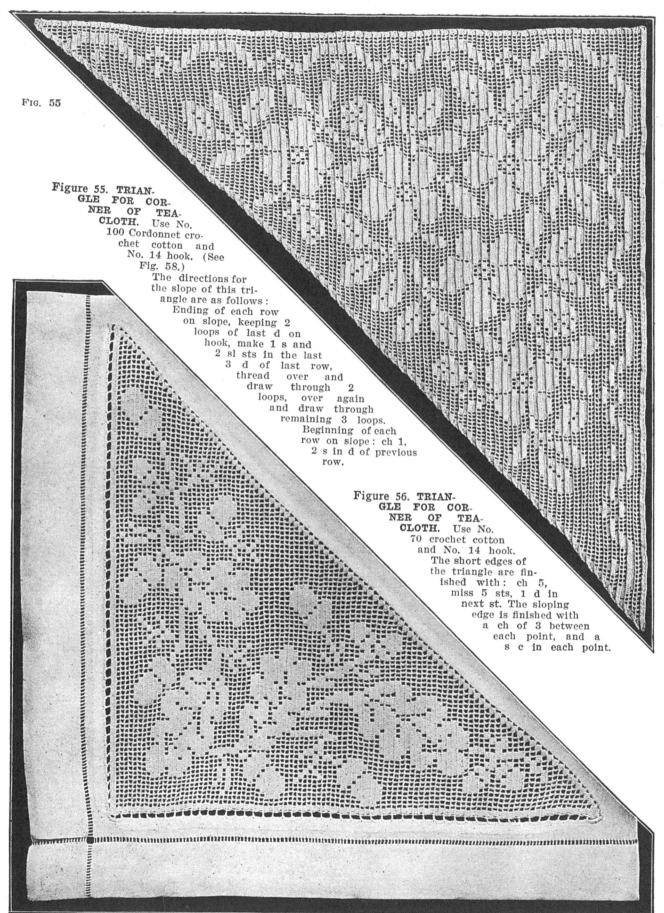

Figure 55. TRIAN-
GLE FOR COR-
NER OF TEA-
CLOTH. Use No.
100 Cordonnet cro-
chet cotton and
No. 14 hook. (See
Fig. 58.)
The directions for
the slope of this tri-
angle are as follows:
Ending of each row
on slope, keeping 2
loops of last d on
hook, make 1 s and
2 sl sts in the last
3 d of last row,
thread over and
draw through 2
loops, over again
and draw through
remaining 3 loops.
Beginning of each
row on slope: ch 1,
2 s in d of previous
row.

Figure 56. TRIAN-
GLE FOR COR-
NER OF TEA-
CLOTH. Use No.
70 crochet cotton
and No. 14 hook.
The short edges of
the triangle are fin-
ished with: ch 5,
miss 5 sts, 1 d in
next st. The sloping
edge is finished with
a ch of 3 between
each point, and a
s c in each point.

FIG. 56. (See directions above)

100 meshes

FIG. 57   87 meshes

B

A

A

FIG. 58. (See Fig. 55)   138 meshes

B

21

Figure 60. TABLE-CLOTH.—This heavy white linen cloth has an insertion of filet crochet worked with No. 100 Cordonnet crochet cotton and a No. 14 hook. The edge is hemstitched and the insertion is put in with rolled hems. After the crochet is finished shrink it thoroughly. Then the linen, also thoroughly shrunk, is to be cut and fitted to the crochet.

To work the insertion, Fig. 62, make 1149 chain. Refer to the diagram, Fig. 60, and begin at A. Work 41 rows, ending at B. Turn, and work 299 short rows, according to Fig. 62, ending at E. Cut thread and fasten at F. Work the third side of the insertion like the second, ending at K. From here, a chain of 902 is made and its end fastened at E. The thread is again cut and joined at L. The last side is then worked like the first, according to Fig. 62.

Figure 59. IMITATION HEMSTITCH IN CROCHET FOR TOWELS, ETC.—This pretty crochet will be found very attractive for the opposite end of a towel decorated with filet crochet.

Make a ch of the required length; turn and work singles into each stitch of chain, cut thread and fasten into other end of work; ch 4, 2 t (holding last st of each t on needle, making 3 st in all); draw thread through all and fasten snugly with ch st. * Chain 2, 3 t, holding last st of each on needle (making 4 in all); draw thread through all and fasten snugly with ch st. * Repeat between * for length of work. Cut thread, and beginning at other end of work make 3 singles in each open space. When sewing the crochet into the towel the open edge should always be sewed in first, otherwise the work will not be even. The model was done with No. 70 crochet cotton and a No. 14 hook.

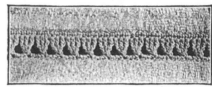

FIG. 59. CROCHET HEMSTITCH

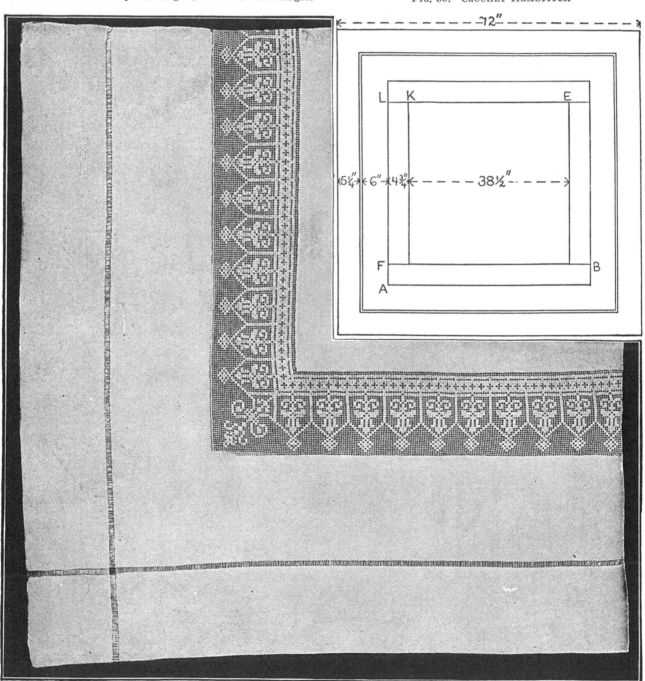

FIG. 60. CORNER OF TABLE-CLOTH AND DIAGRAM FOR WORKING. (See Fig. 62)

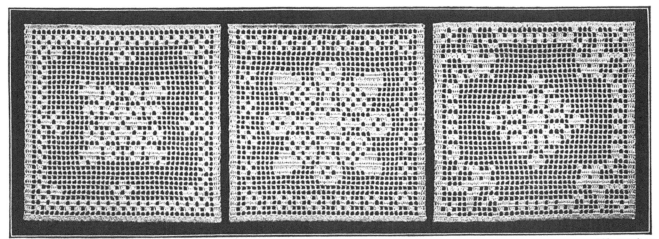

FIG. 61   39 meshes

Squares in filet crochet like those shown in Fig. 61 have many and varied uses. They may be finished with a picot edge and used as doilies, and four or nine squares joined make a nice centrepiece.

They may be used together for an all-lace bedspread or joined with alternate squares of plain or embroidered linen. The linen could be French-hemmed or hemstitched, and a touch of color added in simple outline embroidery or cross-stitch. Crochet squares are lovely inserted in the ends of towels, when made small, in the corners of table-covers, or used as borders of insertion around square cloths.

FIG. 62. REDUCED SECTION OF CROCHET FOR TABLE-CLOTH. (See Fig. 60)

FIG. 63.   (See Fig. 68)
The model was worked with No. 70 Cordonnet cotton and No. 14 hook

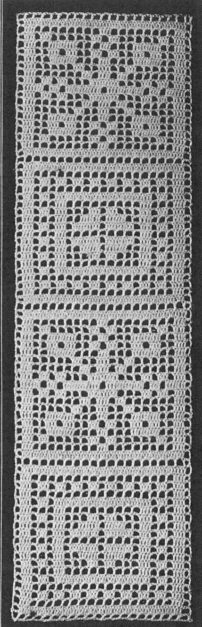

FIG. 66   21 meshes

A bedspread made of strips of crochet like Fig. 66 and plain linen is very attractive; and the lily edging and insertion used in the same way work up into an exquisite spread.

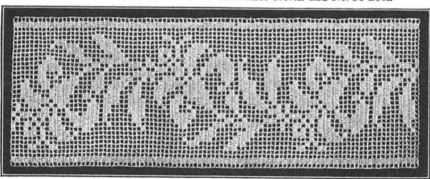

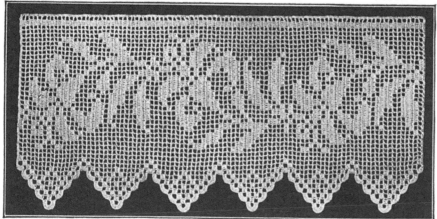

FIGS. 64, 65. EDGING AND INSERTION

33 meshes

FIG. 67   33 meshes

FIG. 68. (See Fig. 63) SPRING 91 x 127 meshes

The panel above and the one called "Autumn," on page 27, are both suitable for pillow-tops, chair-backs, door-panels, and bedspreads. For a pillow, insert the crocheted panel in linen, which may be either plain or embroidered, and finish the edges with a filet crochet edging or Cluny lace. The size of the panel when finished will be governed by the thread used. (See page 3 for the number of meshes to an inch in threads of different sizes.) When the panels are made for chair-covers a nice finish for the edges is a row of plain double crochet with picots, or a simple picot edging.

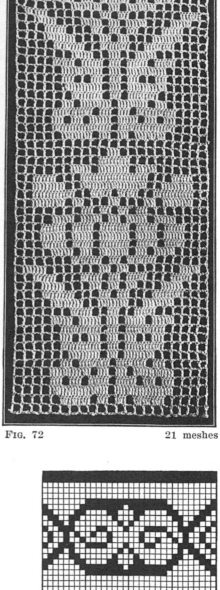

FIG. 69. (See Fig. 75.)   The model was worked with No. 70 Cordonnet cotton and No. 14 hook

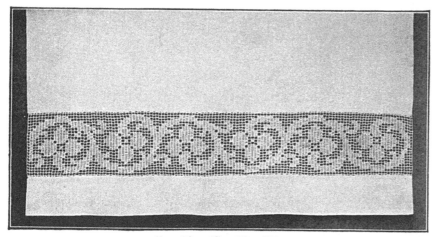

FIG. 70.   (See Fig. 71)

FIG. 72   21 meshes

FIG. 71. (See Fig. 70)   21 meshes

FIG. 73. (See Fig. 74)   24 meshes

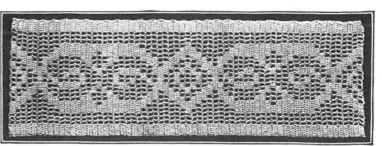

FIG. 74.   (See Fig. 73)

FIG. 75. (See Fig. 69) AUTUMN 91 x 127 meshes

This panel and "Spring," shown on page 25, are very attractive used on bedspreads, inset in the linen and bordered by a filet insertion of the proper width. Another pretty arrangement for a spread is to use either panel in the centre, four crocheted squares in the corners, and on the sides, between the corners, the motto, "Early to Bed," etc., in Cameo crochet, which is given in the Priscilla Bedspread Book with full directions for working. This insertion could also be done in ordinary filet crochet or cross-stitch, as preferred. The two designs could be adapted for door-panels.

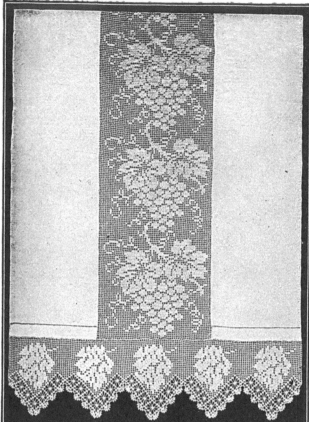

FIG. 76. (See Fig. 77 and directions for Edging)

FIG. 77. (See Fig. 76)   62 meshes

Figure 76. EDGING FOR SCARF.—Chain (ch) 72.

1st row—Double crochet (d) in 9th ch from hook and make 21 more spaces (sp) (2 ch, d in 3d ch), 4 d in last 4 ch; turn.

2d row—Chain 11, 1 d into each of 9th, 10th, and 11th ch from hook and 1 d into next d, ch 2, 4 d in sp after 4 d of 1st row, 21 sp; turn.

3d row—Chain 5, 1 d in 1st d (for 1 sp), 19 more sp, 4 d, ch 5, 1 treble (t) over 2 ch between two groups of d, ch 5, 4 d into loop at end of row; turn.

4th row—Chain 11, 1 d into each of the 9th, 10th, and 11th ch from hook and 1 d into next d, ch 5, 3 s c over t of last row, using 1 ch at each side of t, ch 5, 4 d, 19 sp; turn.

5th row—Chain 5, 1 d in 1st d (this will hereafter be included in the number of sp beginning the row), 3 more sp. 4 d, 13 sp, 4 d, ch 5, 5 s c over 3 s c of last row, using 1 ch at each side, ch 5, 4 d into loop; turn.

6th row—Chain 11, 1 d into 9th, 10th, and 11th ch and 1 d into next d, ch 2, 4 d over 5 ch, ch 5, 3 s c over 5 s c, ch 5, 4 d over 5 ch, 13 sp, 4 d, 5 sp; turn.

7th row—Five sp, 4 d, 6 sp, 7 d, 6 sp, 4 d over 5 ch, ch 4, 1 t in 3 s c, ch 4, 4 d over 5 ch, ch 5, 1 t over 2 ch, ch 5, 4 d in loop; turn.

8th row—Chain 11, 1 d in 9th, 10th, and 11th ch, 1 d in d, ch 5, 3 s c, ch 5, 4 d over 4 ch, ch 2, 4 d over 4 ch, 4 sp, 4 d, 1 sp, 13 d, 4 sp, 4 d, 6 sp; turn.

9th row—Six sp, 4 d, 3 sp, 25 d, 4 sp, 4 d, ch 5, 5 s c, ch 5, 4 d in loop; turn.

10th row—Chain 11, 1 d in 9th, 10th, and 11th ch, 1 d in d, ch 2, 4 d over 5 ch, ch 5, 3 s c, ch 5, 4 d, 5 sp, 13 d, 1 sp, 13 d, 2 sp, 4 d, 6 sp; turn.

11th row—Seven sp, 13 d, 2 sp, 13 d, 3 sp, 10 d, 1 sp. 4 d, ch 4, 1 t in s c, ch 4, 4 d over 5 ch, ch 5, 1 t over 2 ch, ch 5, 4 d in loop; turn.

12th row—Chain 11, 1 d in 9th, 10th, and 11th ch, 1 d in d, ch 5, 3 s c, ch 5, 4 d, ch 2, 4 d, 3 sp, 13 d, 3 sp, 10 d, 3 sp, 4 d, 1 sp, 10 d, 4 sp; turn.

13th row—Three sp, 25 d, 1 sp, 16 d, 1 sp, 16 d, 3 sp, 4 d, ch 5, 5 s c, ch 5, 4 d in loop; turn.

14th row—Chain 11, 1 d in 9th, 10th, and 11th ch, 1 d in d, ch 2, 4 d over 5 ch, ch 5, 3 s c, ch 5, 4 d, 2 sp, 37 d, 1 sp, 4 d, 1 sp, 16 d, 5 sp; turn.

15th row—Four sp, 13 d, 2 sp, 7 d, 2 sp, 13 d, 1 sp, 22 d, 2 sp, 4 d, ch 4, 1 t over s c, ch 4, 4 d over 5 ch, ch 5, 1 t over 2 ch, ch 5, 4 d in loop; turn.

16th row—Chain 11, 1 d in 9th, 10th, and 11th ch, 1 d in d, ch 5, 3 s c over t, ch 5, 4 d over 4 ch, ch 2, 4 d over 4 ch, 4 sp, 22 d, 5 sp, 16 d, 2 sp, 10 d, 3 sp; turn.

17th row—Three sp, 31 d, 1 sp, 19 d, 3 sp, 13 d, 3 sp, 4 d, ch 5, 5 s c, ch 5, 4 d; turn.

18th row—Chain 5, 4 d over 5 ch, ch 5, 3 s c, ch 5, 4 d, ch 2, 4 d in sp, 3 sp, 19 d, 2 sp, 13 d, 2 sp, 7 d, 2 sp, 13 d, 4 sp; turn.

19th row—Five sp, 7 d, 1 sp, 16 d, 1 sp, 28 d, 5 sp, 4 d, ch 5, 1 t over 2 ch, ch 5, 4 d in 5 ch, ch 4, 1 t over s c, ch 4, 4 d over 5 ch; turn.

20th row—Chain 5, 4 d over 4 ch, ch 2, 4 d over 4 ch, ch 5, 3 s c over t, ch 5, 4 d in sp, 2 sp, 10 d, 2 sp, 16 d, 1 sp, 34 d, 3 sp; turn.

21st row—Four sp, 13 d, 2 sp, 16 d, 1 sp, 7 d, 1 sp, 13 d, 3 sp, 4 d, ch 5, 5 s c, ch 5, 4 d; turn.

22d row—Chain 5, 4 d over 5 ch. ch 5, 3 s c, ch 5, 4 d over 5 ch, ch 2, 4 d, 3 sp, 7 d, 1 sp, 10 d, 1 sp, 13 d, 2 sp, 7 d, 7 sp; turn.

23d row—Four sp, 22 d, 1 sp, 16 d, 1 sp, 16 d, 1 sp, 4 d, ch 5, 1 t over 2 ch, ch 5, 4 d over 5 ch, ch 4, 1 t over s c, ch 4, 4 d; turn.

24th row—Chain 5, 4 d over 4 ch, ch 2, 4 d over 4 ch, ch 5, 3 s c, ch 5, 4 d, 1 sp, 10 d, 1 sp, 25 d, 1 sp, 13 d, 5 sp; turn.

25th row—Six sp, 10 d, 1 sp, 22 d, 2 sp, 7 d, 1 sp, 4 d, ch 5, 5 s c, ch 5, 4 d over 5 ch; turn.

26th row—Chain 5, 4 d over 5 ch, ch 5, 3 s c, ch 5, 4 d over 5 ch, ch 2, 4 d, 1 sp, 7 d, 2 sp, 16 d, 2 sp, 7 d, 7 sp; turn.

27th row—Eight sp, 4 d, 3 sp, 7 d, 3 sp, 7 d, 1 sp, 4 d, ch 5, 1 t over 2 ch, ch 5, 4 d over 5 ch, ch 4, 1 t over s c, ch 4, 4 d; turn.

28th row—Chain 5, 4 d over 4 ch, ch 2, 4 d over 4 ch, ch 5, 3 s c over t, ch 5, 4 d, 4 sp, 7 d, 13 sp; turn.

29th row—Eighteen sp, 4 d, ch 5, 5 s c, ch 5, 4 d; turn.

30th row—Chain 5, 4 d over 5 ch, ch 5, 3 s c, ch 5, 4 d over 5 ch, 19 sp; turn.

31st row—Twenty sp, 4 d over 5 ch, ch 4, 1 t, ch 4, 4 d; turn. *32d row*—Chain 5, 4 d over 4 ch, ch 2, 4 d over 4 ch, 21 sp. Repeat from beginning.

Edge to Finish.—Fasten thread in 1st d, 3 s c in next 3 d, ch 3, * 3 s c in first loop, ch 1, 6 t with picot (5 ch, s c in 1st ch) between each t in next loop; repeat from * to loop on side of point, ch 1, 6 t with picot between each t in loop on other side of point and continue down side.

Finished scarf is 1 yard 19 inches long without edge. Use No. 50 Cordonnet cotton and No. 12 hook.

FIG. 78. SQUARE WITH ROSE BORDER. OLD SWEDISH DESIGN

Use Cordonnet crochet cotton No. 50 and a No. 12 hook. Make a very snug chain, about a yard in length. At end of this chain make a shell of * 3 d, 3 ch, 3 d for the first corner, then 52 spaces * Repeat from * to * for the three remaining sides. Cut off extra chain, join carefully and proceed with the first row of the pattern, placing shell in shell at each corner, not forgetting to turn the work when starting each new row.

The edge finish consists of 2 s c in each square with 1 s c in each d, while at every 4th d a picot of 5 ch occurs. This finish is used on both inside and outside edges of the border square. A picot is used at each corner.

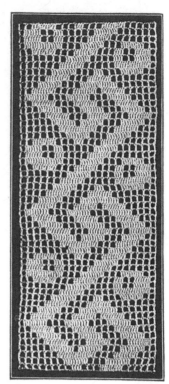

FIG. 79. (See Fig. 81.) Use No. 40 Cordonnet cotton and No. 11 hook

FIG. 80.   20 meshes

FIG. 81. (See Fig. 79)   93 meshes

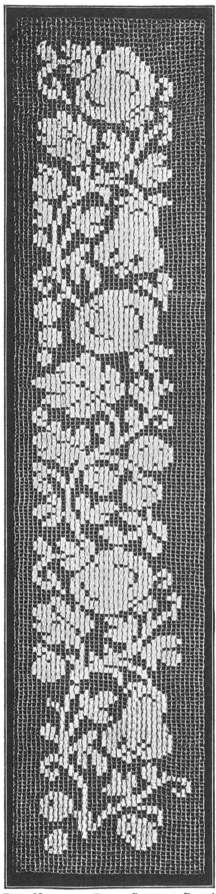

Figures 82 and 86. FILET CROCHET BRODÉ. — This novelty is a step between the old-fashioned Filet Brodé and the Filet Crochet which is an imitation of it. The foundation is crocheted mesh instead of the ordinary netting, and the design is darned in as in Filet Brodé.

Figure 82. — This strip of Filet Crochet Brodé is done in coarse écru thread, about No. 20, and No. 7 hook, the mesh being made with 2 ch, 1 d. The piece is 221 meshes in length and 40 meshes in width. The foundation chain is 126 stitches. The weaving is done in the common filet stitch, *point de reprise,* which is simple weaving back and forth, over and under the mesh. A coarse, soft, white cotton is used for the weaving, which closely fills the mesh.

Figure 86. (See Figs. 83, 84, 85)—The beautiful insertion for the towel is worked with No. 40 Cordonnet crochet cotton and No. 11 hook.

The mesh is made with 3 ch, 1 t. The t is made with 2 loops over the hook, and is worked off in twos, three times. To turn at the end requires 7 ch. The wide insertion is 11 meshes wide, 52 ch for foundation; the narrow insertion is 5 meshes wide; ch 28 for foundation, turn, t in the 12th ch from hook. After the 35th row, 39 ch are added, which widens the row to 13 meshes. The woven letter is 11 meshes high. The weaving in the insertion is done with soft mercerized cotton, in *point de reprise,* and the meshes should be well filled. Finish edges with s c.

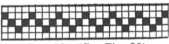

FIG. 83. (See Fig. 86)

FIG. 84. (See Figs. 85, 86)

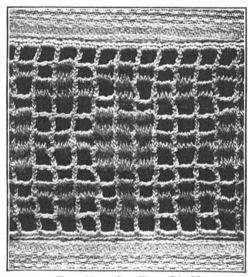

FIG. 85. (See Figs. 84, 86)

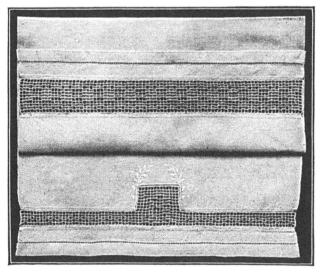

FIG. 82.   FILET CROCHET BRODÉ

FIG. 86. FILET CROCHET BRODÉ.   (See Figs. 83, 84, 85)

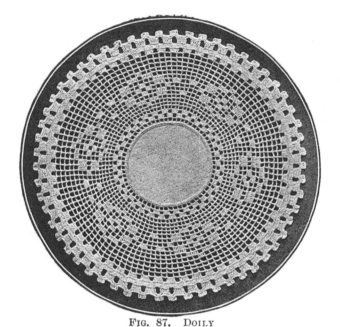

FIG. 87. DOILY

FIG. 88   11 meshes

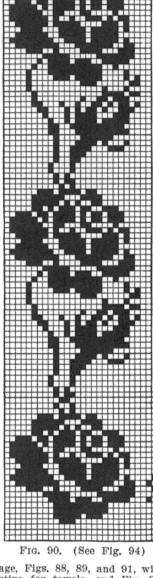

FIG. 89   9 meshes   FIG. 90.   (See Fig. 94)

Figure 87. DOILY. — For this doily (Fig. 87) use No. 70 Cordonnet crochet cotton and a No. 14 hook.

Cut a circle of linen three inches in diameter for the centre of doily, and finish edge with narrow hem. The directions as given require the edge to be sewed to the linen centre, but if desired the work can be begun by crocheting 192 slip stitches through the hem. Chain (ch) 192, join in ring.

1st row—Chain 6, double crochet (d) in third ch, * ch 3, skip 2 ch, d in next stitch (st) *. Repeat between *, making 64 spaces (sp) in row.

2d row—Chain 3, 4 d, * ch 3, 5 d *. Repeat between * around row.

3d row—Chain 3, 4 d in first sp, * ch 3, 5 d in next sp *. Repeat between * around row.

4th row—Chain 6 *, d in third st, ch 3 *, Repeat between *, making 96 sp in row.

5th row—Like 4th row.

6th row—Chain 6, make 5 sp, 4 d in next sp, * 15 sp, 4 d *. Repeat between * until last 9 sp, join with first 6 to complete row.

7th row—Chain 6, 3 sp, * 7 d over 2 sp, 1 sp, 7 d over 2 sp, 11 sp *. Repeat between * and complete as before.

8th row—Chain 6, 1 sp, * 7 d over 2 sp, 5 sp, 7 d over 2 sp, 3 sp, 7 d over 1 sp, 3 sp *. Repeat between *.

9th row—Chain 6, 1 sp, * 7 d, 2 sp, 5 d, 2 sp, 7 d, 8 sp *. Repeat between *.

10th row—Chain 6, * 4 d, 3 sp, 5 d, 1 sp, 5 d, 3 sp, 4 d, 6 sp *. Repeat between *.

11th row—Chain 6, 1 sp, * 7 d over 2 sp, 2 sp, 5 d, 2 sp, 7 d over 2 sp, 2 sp, 7 d over 1 sp, 2 sp, 7 d over 1 sp, 2 sp *. Repeat between *.

12th row—Chain 6, 1 sp, * 7 d, 5 sp, 7 d, 10 sp *. Repeat between *.

13th row—Chain 6, 3 sp, * 7 d over 2 sp, 1 sp, 7 d over 2 sp, 14 sp *. Repeat between *.

14th row—Chain 6, 5 sp, * 4 d over 1 sp, 18 sp. Repeat between *, closing row with 12 sp, which join to the first six.

15th row—Row of sp with ch of 4 in each sp.

16th row—Like 15th row.

17th row—Like 16th row.

18th row—Chain 8, 5 d in first sp, * ch 4, 6 d in next sp but one *. Repeat between *.

19th row—Double crochet over every d (making 4 d in every sp) around row.

20th row—Chain 8, * 6 d, ch 4 *. Repeat between *.

21st row—Single crochet (s) over every d (making 4 s in every sp) around row.

22d row—* Chain 3, 4 d, ch 4 over each sp and 7 s between *. Repeat between *.

NOTE. — The rows begin at right of one of the figures. Join each row evenly. Keep right number of spaces between the figures.

The insertions on this page, Figs. 88, 89, and 91, will be found particularly attractive for towels, and Fig. 95 could serve a like purpose. The stork, Fig. 93, would be charming on a baby pillow.

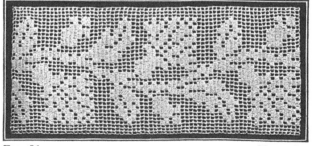

FIG. 91   33 meshes

32

Figure 94. LUNCHEON CLOTH.—Use No. 60 Cordonnet crochet cotton and a No. 12 hook. The model cloth is 40 inches square. The hemstitched hem is 2 inches wide, and beyond that is the crochet insertion, 3¼ inches wide and set in 4 inches from the edge of the cloth. Then comes a strip of linen 3¼ inches wide, followed by the crochet insertion, which is ⅞ of an inch in width. The linen in the centre is 17¼ inches square.

First crochet the two insertions and shrink thoroughly, and after shrinking the linen, cut and fit it to the crochet.

The crochet is in four identical units with the ends joined in the course of the work to form a square. Each unit is 27 spaces wide and 202 spaces long. A little more than one-half a unit (one side) is given in the block pattern, Fig. 90, page 32. When one unit is finished, start the second on the double at the one hundred and ninety-second line.

The inner insertion is worked in the same way, with butted ends, and is 6 spaces wide and 126 spaces long (see Fig. 92).

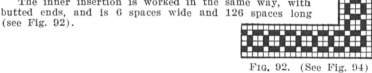

FIG. 92. (See Fig. 94)   FIG. 93   40 meshes

FIG. 94. LUNCHEON CLOTH. (See Figs. 90 and 92)

Figure 96. BURNS' "SELKIRK GRACE" LUNCH CLOTH.

> "Some hae meat that canna eat,
>   An' some wad eat that want it,
>   But we hae meat and we can eat,
>   An' sae the Lord be thankit. Amen."

This familiar verse of the Scotch poet has been very ingeniously arranged for insertion in a lunch cloth, as shown in the illustration.

The crochet in the model cloth was done with No. 50 Cordonnet crochet cotton and a No. 12 hook. The insertion is worked the short way, and is 2¼ inches wide. The hem is 2¾ inches wide, and is hemstitched at the corners. The completed cloth is 45 inches square.

Work one strip and corner of the insertion, then complete the second strip and corner and sew to the first strip, and so on. The block pattern of the insertion is shown in Fig. 97, the letters indicating the connections. If a larger cloth is wanted a coarser cotton should be used.

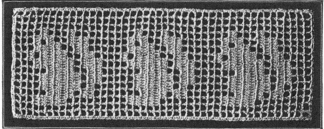

FIG. 95   15 meshes

FIG. 96. BURNS' "SELKIRK GRACE" LUNCH CLOTH. (See Block Pattern, page 35)

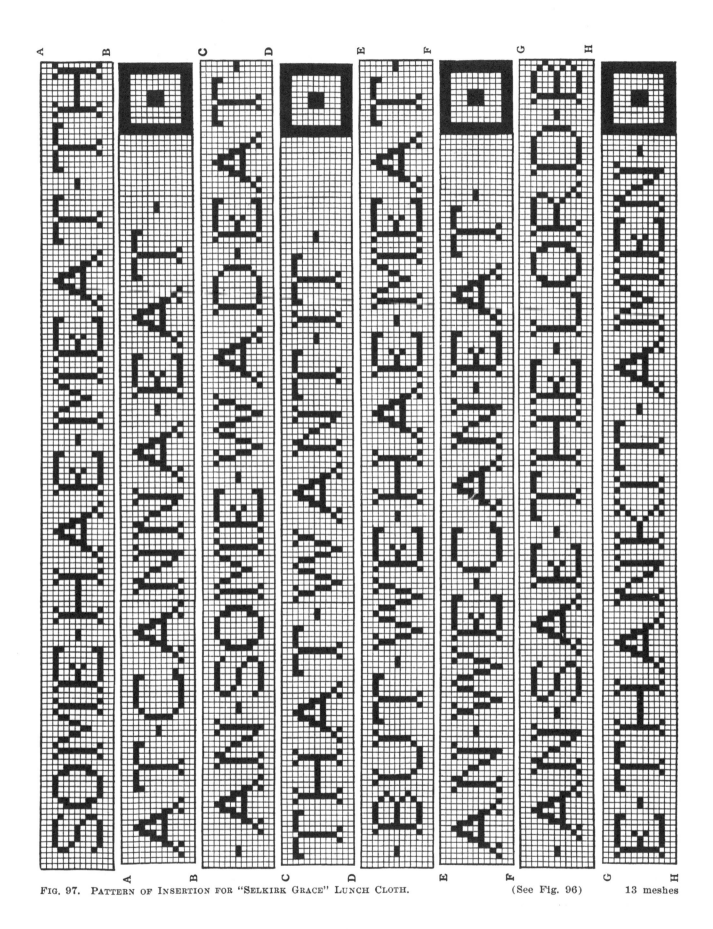

FIG. 97. PATTERN OF INSERTION FOR "SELKIRK GRACE" LUNCH CLOTH.   (See Fig. 96)   13 meshes

Figure 98. TALLEYRAND COFFEE CLOTH. —

    "Doux comme l'amour
      Pur comme un ange
      Noir comme le diable
      Chaud comme l'enfer."

This unique coffee cloth shows Talleyrand's famous lines used as an insertion. The block pattern is shown on this page and the next (Fig. 99), each strip of insertion being 13 rows wide and 169 rows long. The crochet in the model cloth was done with No. 50 Cordonnet crochet cotton and a No. 12 hook. The cloth is 33 inches square, and has a hem 2¾ inches wide, hemstitched at the corners. The insertion is 2¼ inches wide, and is worked the narrow way. Complete one strip and corner, then work second strip and corner and sew to the first strip, and so on. Coarser cotton could be used if a larger cloth is preferred. The letters in the pattern indicate connections.

FIG. 99. PATTERN OF INSERTION FOR COFFEE CLOTH. (See page 37)   13 meshes

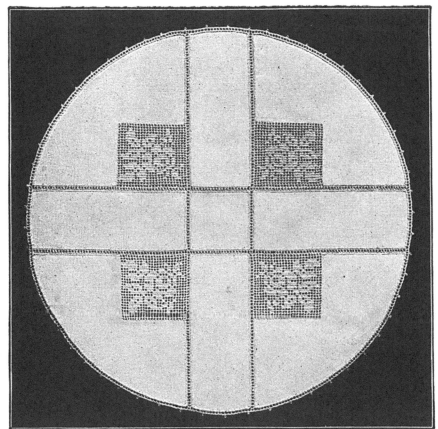

FIG. 100. CENTREPIECE. (See Table, Fig. 101)

S	D	S	D	S	D	S	D	S	D	S	D	S
24												
24												
4	4	12	4	6								
6	4	11	10	3								
3	10	5	10	3	7	5						
5	4	1	7	2	10	3	13	3				
3	7	1	7	1	7	1	4	3	4	1	4	5
4	4	3	4	2	7	1	4	1	4	1	7	4
5	10	1	10	1	7	9						
5	10	1	10	3	4	8						
4	19	2	25	4								
4	10	3	4	1	7	2	4	2	7	3		
1	10	1	10	1	10	2	10	1	4	5		
4	4	1	16	1	10	2	16	2				
11	4	1	7	2	4	1	4	4				
4	4	1	4	2	7	1	10	2	10	4		
2	19	1	13	1	10	1	7	2	4	1		
2	7	1	7	3	13	1	7	1	10	3		
6	4	1	7	1	7	1	10	2	4	4		
3	7	1	4	1	7	4	10	1	10	3		
1	16	1	10	7	4	1	7	3				
2	7	3	4	6	7	2	19					
2	10	3	4	15								
24												
24												

FIG. 101. TABLE FOR WORKING FIG. 100

Figure 100. CENTREPIECE. — This centrepiece of heavy linen has four square insets worked with linen thread No. 40 and a No. 11 hook. The diameter of the centrepiece is 26 inches and the insets are 4½ inches square (see table for working, Fig. 101). The centre strips are 4 inches wide.

To make up, cut a circular paper pattern 26 inches in diameter, and mark on it the two cross strips, 4 inches wide. Cut three patterns—one for quadrant, one for centre square, and one for the half strip; cut the linen by these patterns.

Insert the crochet in the quadrants, allowing for one-quarter-inch hem. Finish edges of all nine pieces with s c, except edge of crochet work. Crochet strips of spaces and sew them to the linen and crochet, thus joining the nine parts as shown in the illustration. Work a row of spaces around the centrepiece, and finish by a row of s c, with a picot every 7 spaces.

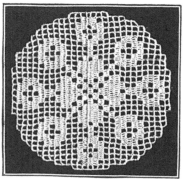

FIG. 102   29 meshes

FIG. 99 — Continued. INSERTION FOR COFFEE CLOTH   13 meshes

Figure 103. BORDER OF TEA CLOTH. *Explanation of Terms.*—Chain (ch). Stitch (st). Slip stitch (sl). Single crochet (s c). Double crochet (d). Treble crochet (t). Space (sp); for a space, ch 2, miss 2, d in next st.

MATERIALS.—Cordonnet crochet cotton No. 40 or 50, steel hook No. 11 or 12.

Begin work at point marked "A" (see Fig. 103) with a ch of 154. The 1st row is worked from outside edge toward inside. Beginning in 4th st from hook, make 7 d in 7 ch, 4 sp, 7 d in next 7 (the given number of d's in a cluster always includes the d at end of last sp), 8 sp, 7 d, 18 sp, 7 d, 8 sp, 7 d, 2 sp, ch 5, turn.

2d row—Double crochet in 2d d, ch 2, 7 d in 7 d, 8 sp over 8 sp, 7 d in 7, 18 sp, 7 d, 8 sp, 7 d, 4 sp, 7 d, turn.

3d row—Slip stitch in each of 7 d, ch 3 (for a d), 6 more d (2 in each sp and 1 in each d between sps), 4 sp, 7 d, 34 sp, 7 d, 4 sp, ch 5, turn.

4th row—Begin with 4 sp and work in d and sps as shown, following design from illustration, turning at ends as described. When the fifth block (blk) on edge is finished (at end of 10th row) ch 10, turn, miss 4 ch, 6 d in next 6 and 1 d in next d; finish row as shown. Begin next blk on edge in same way.

next the st on hook, and sl in next 7 ch. This leaves 2 ch. (If the worker finds the sl on a ch difficult, s c may be substituted with nearly the same effect.) Miss the 2 ch at end, ch 2, d in next d, ch 2, 7 d in 7 d; finish as usual.

At end of next row, after last 4 sp, make 7 d in the 7 sl, ch 9, turn, miss st next st on hook, 6 sl in next 6, miss next 2 ch, 7 d in 7 d; finish as usual.

At end of next row, after sps, d in d next sl, 6 d in 6 sl, ch 9, turn and begin with 6 sl, miss next 2 ch, 7 d in 7 d. Follow design as shown until there are 24 blks on diagonal edge.

For first side of mitred corner, when turning to make 2d row of 24th blk on diagonal edge, ch 3, miss 1 d, 6 d on next 6, 2 sp, 7 d; finish as shown.

Work again to inside edge and after 7 d over the 2 sp, ch 3, turn.

Miss 1 d, 6 d on next 6, 8 sp; finish as shown.

Work again to inside edge, ending with the 4 sp just before last blk on edge, ch 5, turn.

Doubles after first space, 3 sp; finish as shown.

Work again to inside edge, ending with 7 d before last 2 sp on edge.

The next 14 points or "steps" on edge are like the 3d,

Follow design from illustration for 41 rows. The 41st row is worked toward inside edge. The diagonal edge is begun with 42d row. *The chain forming straight edge across corner is not a part of the work now, but is added later.* Follow directions carefully at this point in order to get the blocks across the diagonal corner started right.

After 41st row, ch 10, turn, miss st

having 2 sp at each side of point.

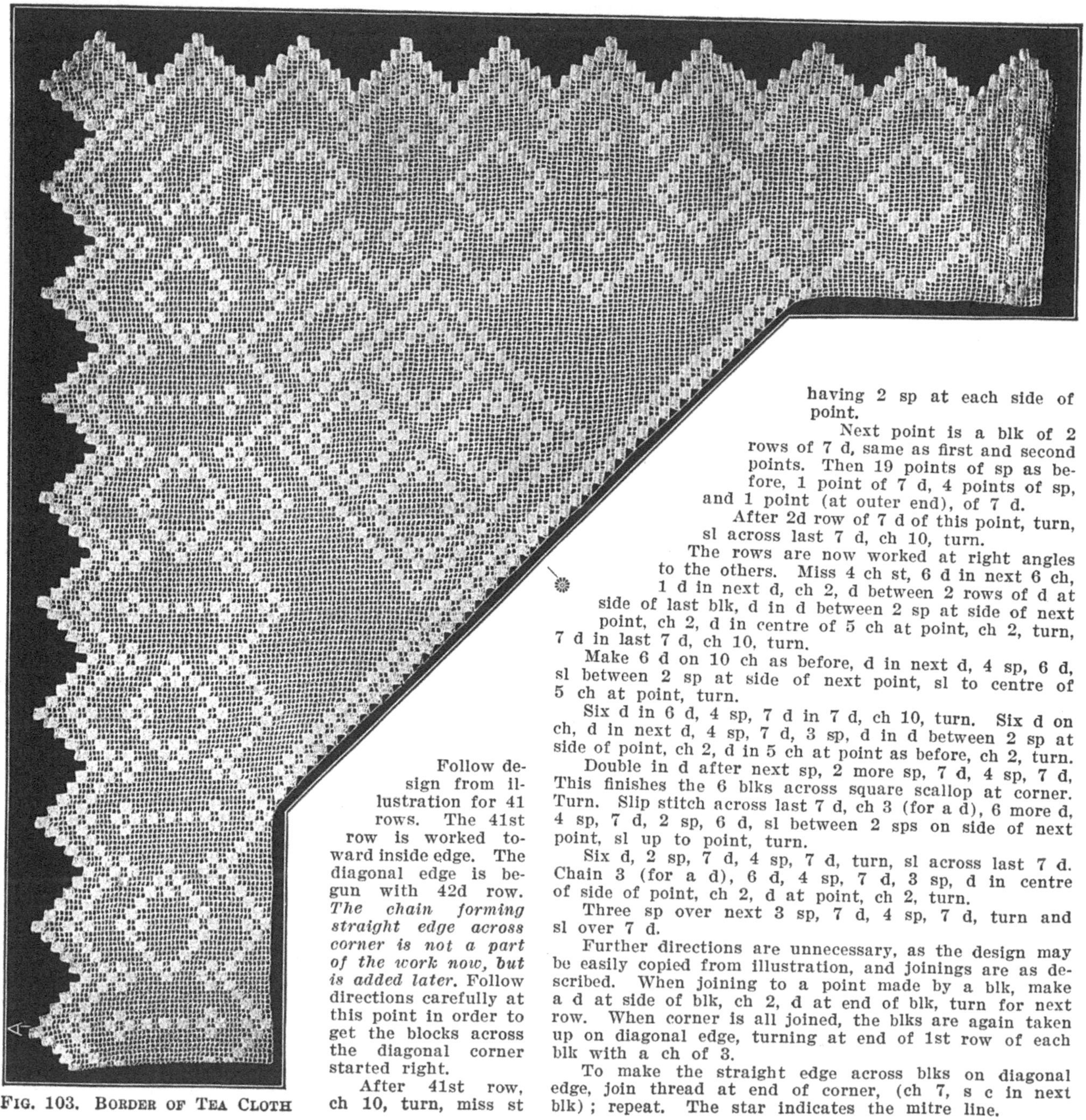

Next point is a blk of 2 rows of 7 d, same as first and second points. Then 19 points of sp as before, 1 point of 7 d, 4 points of sp, and 1 point (at outer end), of 7 d.

After 2d row of 7 d of this point, turn, sl across last 7 d, ch 10, turn.

The rows are now worked at right angles to the others. Miss 4 ch st, 6 d in next 6 ch, 1 d in next d, ch 2, d between 2 rows of d at side of last blk, d in d between 2 sp at side of next point, ch 2, d in centre of 5 ch at point, ch 2, turn, 7 d in last 7 d, ch 10, turn.

Make 6 d on 10 ch as before, d in next d, 4 sp, 6 d, sl between 2 sp at side of next point, sl to centre of 5 ch at point, turn.

Six d in 6 d, 4 sp, 7 d in 7 d, ch 10, turn. Six d on ch, d in next d, 4 sp, 7 d, 3 sp, d in d between 2 sp at side of point, ch 2, d in 5 ch at point as before, ch 2, turn.

Double in d after next sp, 2 more sp, 7 d, 4 sp, 7 d. This finishes the 6 blks across square scallop at corner. Turn. Slip stitch across last 7 d, ch 3 (for a d), 6 more d, 4 sp, 7 d, 2 sp, 6 d, sl between 2 sps on side of next point, sl up to point, turn.

Six d, 2 sp, 7 d, 4 sp, 7 d, turn, sl across last 7 d. Chain 3 (for a d), 6 d, 4 sp, 7 d, 3 sp, d in centre of side of point, ch 2, d at point, ch 2, turn.

Three sp over next 3 sp, 7 d, 4 sp, 7 d, turn and sl over 7 d.

Further directions are unnecessary, as the design may be easily copied from illustration, and joinings are as described. When joining to a point made by a blk, make a d at side of blk, ch 2, d at end of blk, turn for next row. When corner is all joined, the blks are again taken up on diagonal edge, turning at end of 1st row of each blk with a ch of 3.

To make the straight edge across blks on diagonal edge, join thread at end of corner, (ch 7, s c in next blk); repeat. The star indicates the mitre line.

FIG. 103. BORDER OF TEA CLOTH

Figure 104. BORDER OF DOILY.

Explanation of Terms. — Chain (ch). Stitch (st). Slip stitch (sl). Single crochet (s c). Double crochet (d). Treble crochet (t). Space (sp); for a space, ch 2, miss 2, d in next st.

MATERIALS. — Cordonnet crochet cotton No. 40 or 50, steel hook No. 11 or 12. Make 50 ch for foundation.

1st row (see "A," Fig. 105)— Miss 3 ch, d in next 4 ch, 3 sp, 7 d, 2 sp, 7 d, 3 sp, 4 d, 1 sp, ch 8, turn.

2d row—Double crochet in last d of 1st row, 1 sp, 4 d, 3 sp, 7 d, 2 sp, 7 d, 3 sp, 4 d, turn.

3d row—Slip stitch across 4 d, ch 3 (for a d), 2 d in next sp and 1 d in next d, 4 sp, 7 d, 6 sp, 4 d, ch 2, d in 3d of 8 ch, then ch 10, turn.

4th row—Double crochet in 3d ch st (counting back from last d of 3d row) ch 2, d in last d of 3d row, 6 more d, 6 sp, 7 d, 3 sp, 4 d, turn.

5th row—Beginning same as 3d row, finish as shown in illustration, ending with 10 ch.

6th row—Beginning same as 4th row, finish as shown.

7th and 8th rows—Work as shown, and after last 4 d of 8th row, ch 10, turn.

9th row—Miss st next one on hook, sl in next 4, miss next 3, d in next 2, also d in last d of 8th row. Continue with sps and d as shown, finishing row as before.

10th row—Work as shown, after last 4 sp, making 4 d in 4 sl at end, ch 10, turn.

11th row—Beginning same as 9th row, finish as shown.

12th row—Work as shown, ending with 4 d in 4 sl. *13th row*—Chain 6, miss 4 ch, d in next 2 ch and in next d, finish as shown.

Continue working design from illustration (Fig. 105), making edges as directed.

In *17th row* work only to first sp, over last 7 d of 16th row. After first sp ch 5, turn. Work back to outside edge.

The *19th row* ends with first sp over last 7 d of 18th row; ch 5, turn. Continue working as shown in detail of corner (Fig. 105), making outside edge as described for first scallop.

In *39th row* work to first sp over 7 d of 38th row. After this sp, ch 5, turn, d in next d, ch 2, 4 d on edge, turn, sl across 4 d, ch 3, 3 d, ch 10, turn. This finishes half of corner.

To begin next half of corner, miss 1 ch, sl in next 4 ch, miss next 3 ch, d in next 2 ch, and in next d, ch 2, sl in centre of 5 ch at next point, sl across next 2 sp and in next 3 d to corner of 7 d; ch 2, turn, 3 sp over 3 sp of last row, 1 sp over 4 d on edge, 4 d in 4 sl, ch 6, turn. Miss 4 ch, 2 d in next 2, 1 d in next d, 3 sp, 7 d, sl in 5 ch at corner, sl across 2 sp and 3 d, to corner of 7 d. The work shown in detail of corner (Fig. 105) ends at this point. The design may be followed from the cut of completed doily, Fig. 104.

The thread is again joined near the lower edge (Fig. 105) and just enough work done to show method of working the inside edge (where border is joined to centre) on second half of corner.

For extra row on inside edge, join thread to a corner, (ch 3, d in next sp, ch 3, s c in next corner); repeat.

1st row on outside edge—Join in centre between two scallops, ch 3 for a t, 1 t in same place, ch 2, s c in next blk, * ch 4, s c in next blk; repeat from *, making a s c in centre of blk at point, and 2 t between scallops.

2d row—Chain 5, sl back in second ch for a picot, ch 2, s c in next loop; repeat.

This border for doily matches the border of cloth, Fig. 103.

FIG. 104. DOILY TO MATCH TEA CLOTH, FIG. 103. (See detail, Fig. 105)

THREAD. Most of the work in this book was done with Cordonnet crochet cotton. The table on page 3, which gives the size of the thread and of the corresponding hook and the number of meshes per inch, was made upon this basis. The size of thread made by different manufacturers varies. For instance, a No. 40 linen thread is nearly as coarse as a No. 20 cotton thread. Therefore, if crochet is made with any other than Cordonnet cotton, it will probably require a different sized hook and make different sized meshes than are given in the table.

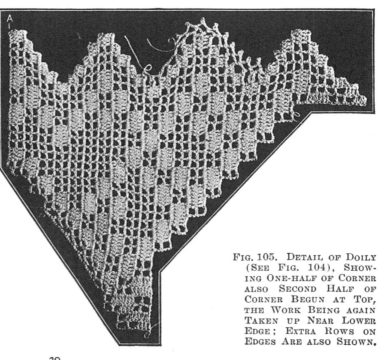

FIG. 105. DETAIL OF DOILY (SEE FIG. 104), SHOWING ONE-HALF OF CORNER ALSO SECOND HALF OF CORNER BEGUN AT TOP, THE WORK BEING AGAIN TAKEN UP NEAR LOWER EDGE; EXTRA ROWS ON EDGES ARE ALSO SHOWN.

**Figure 107. TOWEL WITH INSERTION IN CAMEO CRO-
CHET** (see Fig. 106 and page 3).—This new and beautiful form of filet crochet has the solid portion of the
design worked in color. There must be a separate colored thread carried for every group of blocks in the
row, which are separated by open spaces worked in
white, since the color cannot be carried over the white.

In changing from white to color, ch 2, tie the colored
thread in the top of the next d in previous row; ch 2
with color, pulling the last st of ch through both the
colored loop and the white. When crocheting with the
color, carry the white along, crocheting over it. The white
thread must be pulled tightly or it will show through the
colored stitches. When taking up the white again, the
last colored d is not finished, but the white thread is
pulled through the last two loops of color. The color is
now dropped, to be picked up again on the next row when
the process is repeated. The insertion was worked with
Cordonnet crochet cotton, white No. 40, blue No. 30, and
No. 11 hook. See page 3 for illustration of work in full size.

Figure 108. FLOWER INSERTION. — This design can be
worked from the illustration.

For the scallops, 1 single
crochet in edge, chain 9, miss
2 spaces, single crochet in next;
repeat for entire length of edge;
turn, 4 single crochet, 1 picot, 4
single crochet, in each loop of 9
chain. This charming pattern
would combine prettily with the
floral edging, Fig. 116, page 42,
for towels and scarfs, and the
separate units could be adapted
in many attractive ways.

FIG. 106.   (See Fig. 107)

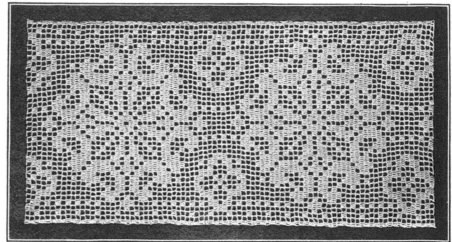

FIG. 109   39 meshes

[CONCLUDED FROM PAGE 3]

on after the pattern is completed. Sometimes the edge of
single crochet is varied by making a picot at every 10th
or 12th stitch.

The ability to crochet *square* should be learned and
cultivated, as resulting in superior work and greater range
of design.

When crocheting for any length of time, the fingers
may become chafed. To avoid this, a good plan is to use
a finger from an old glove.

LAUNDERING.—Although a new piece of work does
not usually need to be laundered, it adds greatly to its
appearance. The crochet should be squeezed, not rubbed,
in good soap-suds. It should then be rinsed well without twisting.

When crochet is to be combined with linen, both the
linen and crochet should be thoroughly shrunk. The crochet is then pinned on the cloth and the cloth cut to
fit the crochet. This is the only way to ensure a perfectly
smooth piece of work.

After a piece is finished, it should be pressed on a thickly
padded board, under a damp cloth.

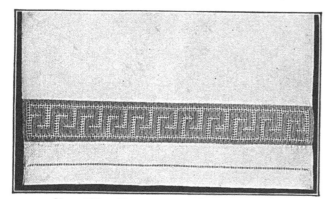

FIG. 107. TOWEL WITH CAMEO CROCHET
(See page 3 and Fig. 106)

Figure 109 is a very handsome insertion that is adapt-
able for a bedspread with alternate strips of linen.

The large unit would also work up into a square and
could be used for a spread with linen squares; a suitable
edging could be arranged from the insertion by the addi-
tion of scallops. The adaptations of the units of designs
are various, and their possibilities should be studied by
workers in search of new combinations.

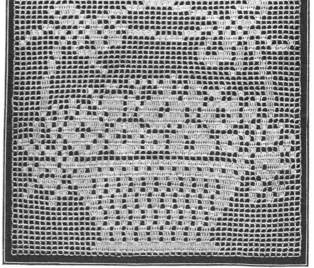

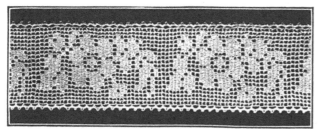

FIG. 108.   (For scallop, see text above)   19 meshes

FIG. 110   49 x 50 meshes

D	S	D	S	D	S	D	S	D	S	D
7	F_2	X	1	7	6	10	3	10	B	F
B	1	B	X	7	4	4	6	7	B_3	7
E_2 7	F_2	X	1	7	10	4	1			
E_4 X	6	10	B_3	7						
E_2 7	F_3	7	3							
E_3 4	1	B_3	X	7						
E_2 7	F_2	C_5	Fasten to beginning of previous row							
4	1	B_2	X	7						
E_2 7	F									
X	B	7	W							
5	F	C_5								

12th row—Seven d in 7 d of previous row, W.

13th row—Five d, F 2, ch 2, 1 d in nearest corner, ch 2, 1 d in nearest angle, 7 d over the one space and 4 d. Chain 2, 1 d, fasten to d one space up from next angle. Chain 2, fasten to next space up. Slip stitch forward over three following spaces. Turn, ch 2, 1 d, forming a space.

D	S	D	S	D	S	D
X	5	10	B_2	7	W	
5	F_2	X	1	7	10	2

Two s c, sl st forward over space and half of block, turn, ch 2, 1 d, forming a space.

D	S	D	S	D	S	D	S	D	S	D	S	D	S	D
7	4	4	6	7	B_2	7	W							
5	F_2	X	1	7	6	10	3	10	F_2					
X	B_2	7	3	7	R	8	6	7	B_2	7	W			
5	F_2	X	1	10	6	4	R	5	R	5	4	10	F	
X	B	7	6	10	8	7	1	B_2	X	7	W			
5	F_3	10	3	10	7	7	3	7	1					
10	2	8	R	4	1	10	1	5	R	10	3	7	B_3	7 W
5	F_4	7	2	9	R	9	1	4	R	5	1	6	R	9 2 7
10	2	8	R	4	1	10	1	5	R	10	3	7	B_4	7
E_2 7	F_3	10	3	10	7	7	3	7	1					
X	B	7	6	10	8	7	1	B_3	X	7				
E_2 7	F_2	X	1	10	6	4	R	5	R	5	4	10	F	
B_2	X	7	3	7	R	8	6	7	B_3	7		Turn		E_2

FIG. 113. TABLE FOR FIG. 111

FIG. 111. DOILY IN FANCY FILET CROCHET
(See Detail, Fig. 112, and Table, Fig. 113)

DESIGNS. Workers wishing to copy or alter patterns for filet crochet, or, having some artistic ability, to make original designs, and finding it tedious to rule a great many squares, may buy paper already ruled. It is sold under the name of cross-section paper, and can be bought where artists' materials are sold.

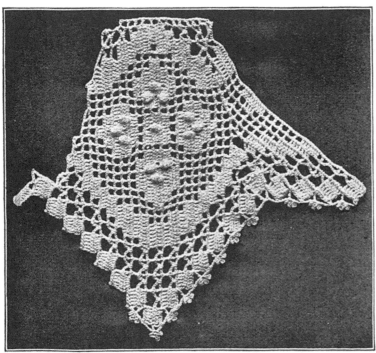

FIG. 112. DETAIL OF DOILY, FIG. 111

The first row of the table begins at the outside edge of the crochet. The last row ends at the outside edge. The crochet was made with Cordonnet crochet cotton No. 20 and hook No. 11.

EDGE. — Fasten at point of scallop, ch 3, 1 t in angle, 3 picots, ch 3, 1 s c in corner, work 6 times down side of scallop, ch 3, 1 t in each angle, ch 3, s c in corner, ch 3, 1 t in angle, 3 p, ch 3, 1 s c in corner, work 6 times up sides of scallop, ch 3, 1 d in middle of point, 3 p, ch 3, 1 s c in corner; repeat.

The blocks in relief are marked R in the Table, and are made as follows: A double, fasten 7 more d in the same place, join top of last d to top of first d with a sl st on the wrong side of the work.

This 16-inch doily has a 5-inch linen centre. The crochet may be worked from the accompanying Table, but the detail, Fig. 112, may prove a sufficient guide for the experienced worker. This detail shows a complete scallop, the method of changing direction, the row of spaces with which the inside edge is finished, and the picot edging used on the scallops. The meaning of the letters in the Table will be found on page 3. The figure with the letter shows the number of times the direction is repeated. Thus: E2 means slip stitch over two spaces, B3 means make three blocks, etc.

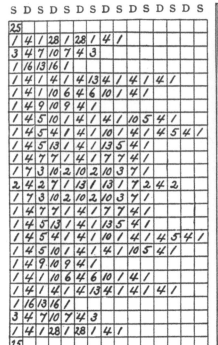

S	D	S	D	S	D	S	D	S	D	S	D	S	D	S
25														
1	4	1	28	1	28	1	4	1						
3	4	7	10	7	4	3								
1	16	13	16	1										
1	4	1	4	1	4	13	4	1	4	1	4	1		
1	4	1	10	6	4	6	10	1	4	1				
1	4	9	10	9	4	1								
1	4	5	10	1	4	1	4	1	10	5	4	1		
1	4	5	4	1	4	1	10	1	4	1	4	5	4	1
1	4	5	13	1	4	1	13	5	4	1				
1	4	7	7	1	4	1	7	7	4	1				
1	7	3	10	2	10	2	10	3	7	1				
2	4	2	7	1	13	1	13	1	7	2	4	2		
1	7	3	10	2	10	2	10	3	7	1				
1	4	7	7	1	4	1	7	7	4	1				
1	4	5	13	1	4	1	13	5	4	1				
1	4	5	4	1	4	1	10	1	4	1	4	5	4	1
1	4	5	10	1	4	1	4	1	10	5	4	1		
1	4	9	10	9	4	1								
1	4	1	10	6	4	6	10	1	4	1				
1	4	1	4	1	4	13	4	1	4	1	4	1		
1	16	13	16	1										
3	4	7	10	7	4	3								
1	4	1	28	1	28	1	4	1						
25														

FIG. 114. TABLE FOR FIG. 118

FIG. 117   113 meshes

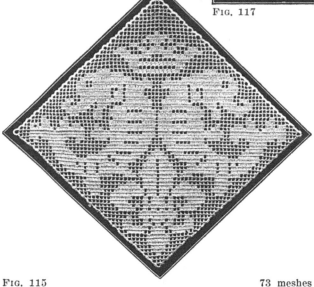

FIG. 115   73 meshes

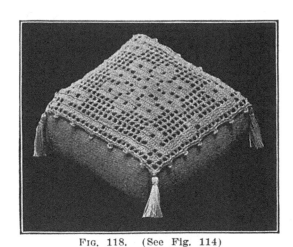

FIG. 118. (See Fig. 114)

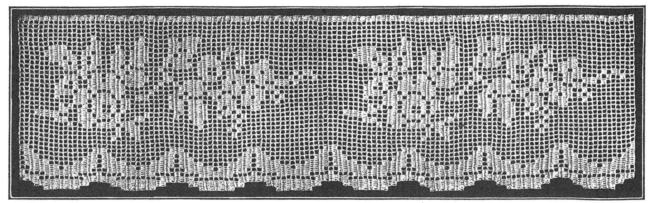

FIG. 116   38 meshes

Figure 122.   TOWEL WITH EMBROIDERED CROCHET.
(See Figs. 119 and 121.) The crochet insertion for this towel is worked according to the design, Fig. 119. Use No. 30 Cordonnet crochet cotton and No. 11 hook.

The model is embroidered with colored mercerized cotton, as shown in Fig. 121, the coloring being as follows: In the centre of the medallion work a flower in French knots, one yellow French knot in the centre, with seven of the same shade around it, and twelve of a lighter shade around those. The illustration, Fig. 121, shows how the green leaves are placed, these being done in chain-stitch caught down with a short stitch over the loop at the end. Smaller French-knot flowers, blue, pink, and lavender, with yellow centres, are worked in the middle of each of the three solid figures that are grouped together. On the two-inch hem of the towel there is a design of the same flowers with stems in outline. The hem is double hemstitched and the same on both ends of the towel.

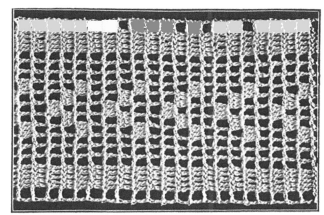

Fig. 120½   15 meshes

In the above insertion, Fig. 120½, a slight variation from the usual filet crochet is shown in the wide mesh of 5 d, forming the horizontal stripe at the top and bottom of the design. But the working of the pattern without mistake has been made possible by the reproduction of the work in full size, thus making the counting of the stitches an easy matter. The insertion will be found very attractive for towels, and if done in carpet warp would be handsome for a bedspread.

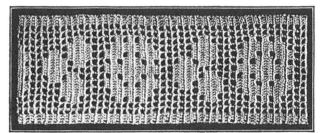

FIG. 119. PATTERN OF FIG. 122   15 meshes

FIG. 120   87 meshes

FIG. 121. INSERTION FOR TOWEL, FIG. 122

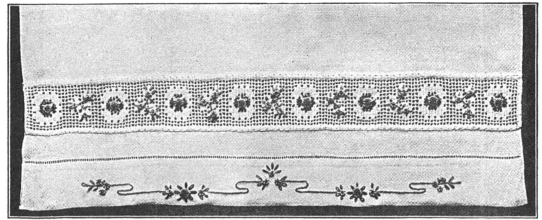

FIG. 122. TOWEL WITH EMBROIDERED CROCHET.   (See Figs. 119 and 121)

Figure 1. TEA CLOTH. (Frontispiece.) *Materials.* — Cordonnet crochet cotton No. 100, hook No. 14, and linen for centre. Shrink linen and crochet, then hem-stitch a square to fit edging. The triangles may be buttonholed to the linen or closely whipped, as preferred.

EXPLANATION OF TERMS.—*Chain* (ch). *Stitch* (st). *Slip stitch* (sl). *Single crochet* (s c). *Double crochet* (d). *Treble crochet* (t). *Space* (sp); for a "space", ch 2, miss 2, d in next st. *Long space* (l sp); for a "long space," ch 5, miss 5 (if over a festoon miss festoon), d in next. *Festoon* (fest); for a festoon, if over a long space, ch 3, s c in long space, ch 3, d in next d; if festoon is over a ch or over doubles, ch 3, miss 2, single in next, ch 3, miss 2, d in next. *Block* (blk). A chain of 3 before a cluster of doubles equals 1 d; thus "3 ch, 6 d," are counted as 7 d in working next row. Both in triangles and edging in working doubles into doubles only the back thread of stitch is taken up, except in working inside edge of edging when both threads are taken up.

Figure 123. INSERTED TRIANGLE. (See Fig. 124.)— Chain 7, turn.

1st row—Double crochet in 4th from hook and in next 2 ch, ch 7, turn.

2d row—Four d in 4 d, ch 3, turn, (3 ch and 3 d count as 4 d in 1st row).

3d row—Miss 1 d, 3 d in next 3 d, 2 d under next 2 of 7 ch, 1 d into next ch st, ch 2, t in same st with last d, ch 7, turn.

4th row—* Double crochet in t, 1 sp, 7 d, * ch 3, turn.

5th row—Miss 1 d, 3 d in next 3, 1 sp, * 7 d, (last 3 made as in 3d row,) ch 2, t in st with last d, ch 7, turn.

6th row—From * to * of 4th row, 1 sp, 4 d, ch 3, turn.

7th row—Miss first d, 6 d, 2 sp, from * to end of 5th row.

8th row—From * to * of 4th row, 2 sp, 7 d, ch 3, turn.

9th row—Twelve more d, 2 sp, from * to end of 5th row.

10th row—From * to * of 4th row, 2 sp, 7 d, 1 sp, 4 d, ch 3, turn.

11th row—Six d, 1 fest, 7 d, 2 sp, from * to end of 5th row.

12th row—From * to * of 4th row, 2 sp, 7 d, one 1 sp (ch 5, miss fest, d in next d), 1 sp, 4 d, ch 3, turn.

13th row—Six d, 2 fest, 7 d, 2 sp, from * to end of 5th row.

Continue working in same way until there are 13 fest in 35th row. In 36th row there are 13 l sp.

The figure of design is begun in the 37th row.

37th row—Make edge as usual, then 8 fest, 19 d (making 5 d in each 1 sp and 1 in each d), 3 fest; finish lower edge as usual.

38th row—Edge, 3 l sp, 19 d, 8 l sp, edge.

39th row—Edge, 5 fest, 7 d, 1 fest, 7 d, 6 sp, 7 d, 1 fest, 7 d, 1 fest, edge.

40th row—Edge, one l sp, 7 d, one l sp, 7 d, 6 sp, 7 d, one l sp, 7 d, 5 l sp, edge.

The design may readily be followed from the illustration from this point. The last row (88th) being made entirely of d's. Work across diagonal side with s c.

Figure 126. EDGING. (See Fig. 125.)—Begin at "A." (See Fig. 126.) Chain 143, turn.

1st row (*worked from outside edge to inside*)—Double in fourth st from hook and in next 5, 2 sp, 7 d, 19 fest, 7 d, ch 3, turn.

2d row—Miss 1 d, 3 d in next 3, 1 sp, 19 l sp, 7 d, 2 sp, 7 d, ch 8, turn.

3d row—* Miss 3 ch st next hook, 5 d in next 5, 1 d in next d, 2 sp, 7 d, * 20 fest, 7 d, ch 3, turn.

4th row—Three d (as in 2d row), 1 sp, 20 l sp, 7 d, 2 sp, 7 d, ch 8, turn.

5th row—From * to * of 3d row, 5 fest, 55 d, (make 5 d in each l sp and 1 in each d), 7 fest, 7 d, ch 3, turn.

6th row—Three d, 1 sp, 7 l sp, 55 d, 5 l sp; finish same as 4th row.

Continue working design from illustration and making edges as described. After 16th row, ch 3, turn, and work 6 d, 2 sp, 7 d over those of preceding row. Continue in same way until there are 6 rows of d across point. After 6th row, turn, sl across last 7 d, ch 3, 6 d, 2 sp, 7 d; finish as shown. Turn after 23d row and sl across 7 d and work as before.

At end of 31st row begin mitred corner. Make only 4 d at lower end of 31st row instead of the usual 7, turn and sl back over the 4 d, ch 8, turn.

32d row—Double crochet in next d (after next fest), one more l sp, 7 d (including the d after sp); finish as shown.

33d row—Work through last 7 d of row, then 1 fest, ch 8, turn.

34th row—Seven d in 7 d; finish as shown.

35th row—Work through last 7 d of row, 1 fest, ch 8, turn.

36th row—Same as 34th row. *37th row*—Same as 35th row.

38th row—Same as 34th row. *39th row*—Same as 35th row.

40th row—Same as 34th row. *41st row*—Same as 35th row.

42d row—Same as 34th row.

43d row—After last 25 d of row, 1 fest, ch 8, turn.

44th row—Twenty-five d in 25 d; finish as shown.

45th row—After last 4 fest, ch 8, turn.

46th row—Double crochet in next d, 3 more l sp; finish as shown.

Work next 6 rows from illustration, turning at inside edge as described for 34th and 35th rows.

57th row—Ends with 7 d, ch 3, turn.

58th row—Miss 1 d, 6 d in next 6; finish as shown.

59th row—Ends with 19 d, ch 3, turn.

61st row—Ends with 5 fest, ch 8, turn, d in next d; finish as shown.

63d row—After 3 fest, ch 8, turn.

65th row—After 1 fest, ch 8, turn.

67th row—After 2 sp, ch 5, turn.

68th row—Double crochet in next d, 1 more sp, 7 d, turn, and sl back over 7 d. This completes first half of corner.

To finish the corner begin as follows:

1st row—Chain 8, turn, miss 3 ch next hook, 5 d in next 5, sl in d between 2 sp, sl in next 3 ch, (to corner of point), turn.

2d row—Six d in 6 d (counting 3 ch as 1 d), ch 8, turn.

3d row—Five d on ch as in 1st row, 1 d in next d, 2 sp, 6 d, sl in 3d of 8 ch forming next point, sl in next 3 ch sts, turn.

4th row—Six d in 6 d, 2 sp, 7 d, ch 8, turn.

5th row—* Five d as in 1st row, 1 d in next d, 2 sp, 7 d, * 1 fest on next 7 d, ch 3, miss 2, s c in next, ch 3, sl in 3d of 8 ch of next point, sl in next 3 of 8 ch, ch 5, turn.

6th row—Double crochet in next d, ch 5, 7 d in 7 d, 2 sp, 7 d, ch 8, turn.

7th row—From * to * of 5th row (of second half of corner), 3 fest, ch 3, miss 2, s c in next, ch 3, sl in 3d and next 3 of 8 ch of next point, (as in 5th row), ch 5, turn.

8th row—Double crochet in next d, 3 more l sp, 7 d; finish as shown.

9th row—Work through second 7 d, 5 fest; finish same as 7th row, except that the 4 sl sts are made on last 4 of 19 d, ch 5, turn.

10th row—Double crochet in next d, 5 more l sp; finish as shown.

11th row—Ends with 19 d, ch 3, s c between 2 rows of 19 d, ch 3, 4 sl on last 4 of 7 d, ch 5, turn.

12th row—Nineteen d on 19 d; finish as shown.

13th row—Ends with 7 d; then finish as 11th row.

14th row—Seven d in 7 d; finish as shown.

Continue working as shown in the illustration, joining rows worked *inward,* same as 5th, and beginning rows worked *outward* with long space as shown.

The *39th row* ends with a 3 ch and a sl at outer end of the 4 sl (over 4 d) at end of 31st row of first half of corner. Turn and again sl back over the 4 d at end of 31st row, turn.

40th row—One sp, 2 l sp, 7 d, 2 sp, 7 d; finish as shown.

41st row—Work toward inside edge and after last 7 d of row, make 1 fest, 7 d, (the 7 d are made in the sp and across end of 4 d), ch 3, turn.

42d row—Miss 1 d, 3 d in next 3, 1 sp, one l sp, 7 d; finish as shown. This row begins straight edge after corner is finished. From this point the design may be readily copied without directions. After working the first large figure after the one at corner, the second one may be worked from illustration showing corner, if the first one is reversed. That is, the 1st row of second figure is same as last row of first, and so on through entire figure.

The difference between this fancy filet crochet and the ordinary kind is in the background, which is more open and lacy, and while the solid parts are the same, four or some multiple of four, small blocks are always used together, except perhaps on an edge. The large details show very plainly how the work is done and how the corners are mitred.

The triangles may be used for a variety of purposes besides the one suggested here. They may be set into sofa-pillows, scarfs, curtains, and bedspreads, or the entire spread could be made of the triangles joined together. This would be after the fashion of a patchwork quilt, the patches consisting of crocheted triangles.

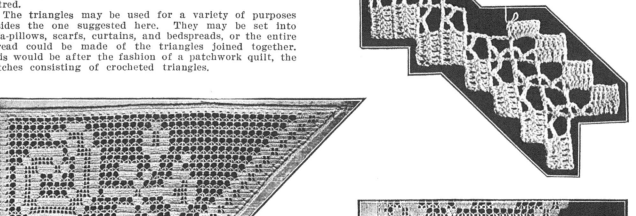

FIG. 125. SMALL SECTION OF INSIDE OF MITRED CORNER OF EDGING, SHOWING METHOD OF JOINING. (See Frontispiece and Fig. 126, also page 44)

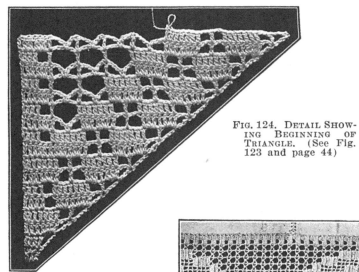

FIG. 123. SECTION OF TRIANGLE, SHOWING ENTIRE FIGURE (See Frontispiece and Detail, Fig. 124, also page 44)

FIG. 124. DETAIL SHOWING BEGINNING OF TRIANGLE. (See Fig. 123 and page 44)

It is quite an easy matter to make an insertion to match the edging, Fig. 126, as this is done by simply disregarding the scallops or points, leaving one row of open meshes below the solid design and finishing off the lower edge exactly like the top.

A beautiful spread can be made of the insertion and edging if heavy linen thread or carpet warp is used. The design is also good for curtains, pillow-scarfs, and any other household linens on which a crocheted edge may be used.

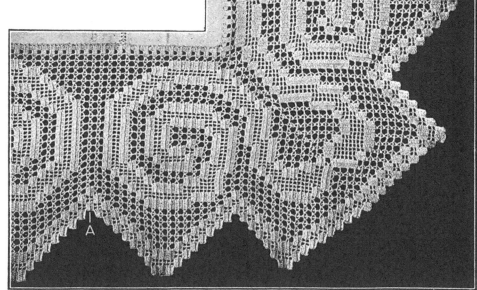

FIG. 126. SECTION OF EDGING FOR TEA CLOTH. (See page 44 and Fig. 125)

Fig. 127. (See Fig. 128)

159 x 97 meshes

FIG. 128. This was worked with No. 70 crochet cotton and No. 14 hook. (See Fig. 127)

Figure 131.   BABY SHOES. (See Figs. 129 and 130.) *Materials.*—One ball Cordonnet crochet cotton No. 150 and No. 14 hook. The two uppers and two soles are made separately and joined with d. The left shoe is given in Fig. 129, and the left sole in Fig. 130; the right upper and sole are made in the same way, and reversed when they are crocheted together.

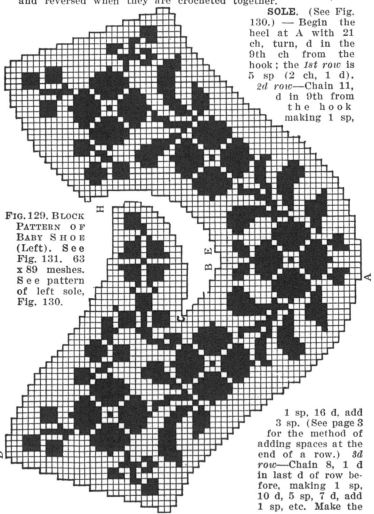

FIG. 129. BLOCK PATTERN OF BABY SHOE (Left). See Fig. 131. 63 x 89 meshes. See pattern of left sole, Fig. 130.

SOLE. (See Fig. 130.) — Begin the heel at A with 21 ch, turn, d in the 9th ch from the hook; the *1st row* is 5 sp (2 ch, 1 d). *2d row*—Chain 11, d in 9th from the hook making 1 sp,

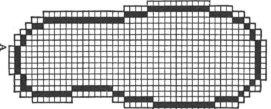

FIG. 130. PATTERN OF LEFT SOLE OF BABY SHOES 20 x 45 meshes. (See Figs. 129 and 131)

second sole like the first, and reverse it in joining to the upper.

UPPER. (See Fig. 129.)—Begin at A, ch 27, turn, d in 9th ch from hook. *1st row*—Seven sp. *2d row*—Chain 18, d in 9th from hook, making 4 sp, 7 sp over 1st row, add 4 sp at the end of the row, etc.

Working back and forth, when B is reached, turn and make 7 rows between B and C. At C, ch 9 for the foundation of next 3 sp, ch 9 more and d into the 9th of the first ch; this will make the first of the 6 sp beyond C. The d will lie across the top of the sp, leaving the hook at the upper right-hand corner of the sp, turn the work and add 5 sp. This makes altogether 6 sp. Then ch 15, turn, d in 9th and make 3 sp over the ch, 6 sp over 6 sp, 3 sp over ch, and 3 sp over the body of the work. 7 d, etc. When D is reached, fasten and cut the thread; join it at E and work back and forth to F. Along the top of the upper (from D to F)

1 sp, 16 d, add 3 sp. (See page 3 for the method of adding spaces at the end of a row.) *3d row*—Chain 8, 1 d in last d of row before, making 1 sp, 10 d, 5 sp, 7 d, add 1 sp, etc. Make the

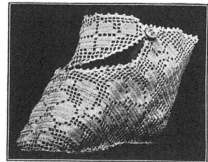

FIG. 131. BABY SHOE. (See Figs. 129 and 130)

FIG. 132. 93 meshes

work 3 s c in each sp along the edge, making a picot of 4 ch after every 6 sts. At H, ch 12 for a buttonhole-loop and cover with s c. Sew a tiny pearl button on the point opposite. With needle and thread, overcast the back seam of the upper, then holding the lower edge of upper to edge of sole, s c both edges together with 3 s c in each sp.

FIG. 133. PANEL SUITABLE FOR A PILLOW. (Worked with No. 70 crochet cotton and No. 14 hook.) 123 x 93 meshes

48

THE END